D1264300

What They DON'T Teach You About Money In the Military!

Personal financial techniques for our Armed Forces personnel, from Recruits to Retirees!

By

Arthur J. Vangeli, CFP®

Published by
Joe Mann Books
Las Vegas, NV 89142

For large quantity book purchases and special group discounts, please contact the publisher at Discounts@ArmedForcesFunds.com

Library of Congress Control Number: 2005903115

ISBN 0-9720392-8-7

First edition, First Printing

Printed in the United States by Morris Publishing
3212 East Highway 30
Kearney, NE 68847
1-800-650-7888

DEDICATION

FOR SHIPMATES, SOLDIERS, and AIRMEN EVERYWHERE, past, present, and future.

For active duty personnel, what you do matters because it changes lives. For retirees, what you did matters because it continues to change lives. Freedom isn't free.

In the big scheme of things, money ranks way, way behind the freedom you provide. Hopefully you'll find some tips on money within these pages thanks solely to the free market system you protect everyday. No one deserves it more.

Additional Acknowledgements

Without the following, this book is simply not possible: Mom & Dad, Debbie & Jeff, Kathy, Mario, Lindy, Tina & Kevin, Aleida & Adrianna, Aunt Rainy & Uncle John, Danielle & Brent, Grover, Denny & Wendy (& Denny III), Capt & Mrs. Johnson, and Fred, Don, Al, Vince, Harry, Mick, Stan, Joe, Tip, Greg, Hap, Merle, Muffet, Warren, Sam, Peter, SmartMoney magazine, American Century, Scottrade, Admiral Boorda, Fred, Laurie, Strom, Grover, Matt, Denny, the Jolly Johnsons, Maiko, Adrianna (Ancient), Clay, Sandy, Russ, Georgette, Jerry, Patt, George, Jim, Mary, Karen, Pat, Naomi, Guy, Joel, Mike, Barbara, Allan, Jarrod, JJ, Mark, Jim, Strom, Carey, Claire, Kim, Danny, Roni, Danielle, Elena, Jim, Laura, Linda, Isabel, Matt, Mike, Ray, Mitch, Kent, Donna, Freddie, Mark, Kimberly, Kat, Evelyn, Top, Harue, Patti, Sandy, John, Gail, Fido the Spider, Hank, Kimberly, Mark, Konan, Lucky, Dottie, and Celeste.

Preface

Thanks For Your Feedback...And Keep It Coming!!!

Thank you, thank you, thank you all for your insightful, resourceful, helpful, and, at times, blunt feedback that you extended via email. As promised, this edition addresses the concerns, areas, and topics that YOU want to know more about. As promised, this edition focuses directly on your feedback.

A special 'thank you' is extended to those of you who took time to comment on Amazon.com's website on the previous version of "Stop Buying $63 Hamburgers!" Your feedback helped us achieve a rare coup in these internet times – a book with more than 25 reviewers that still has a perfect overall five-star rating!!!!! Unheard of, exemplary, but mainly it is a reflection on those who took time and effort to share their satisfaction. Thank you!

Between July 2002 and March 2004 we received more than 8,200 emails from over 2,600 readers! Your commitment to improving this book motivates us all to keep moving forward. The revisions you see between the last version and this version must be attributed to the comments and suggestions you forwarded. Keep it up.

Please note our new 'section' format, addressing the **four major phases** of military life: initial years, re-enlistment decisions, pre-retirement planning, and post-career finances. This new approach is a direct result of your feedback; we hear you loudly and clearly. Your comments leaned decisively toward overall financial planning techniques to keep you informed throughout, and after, your careers. Please note the symbolic aviation terminology linked to each phase of your finances:

Departure
Mission
Approach
Arrival

We invite you to look ahead to anticipate the next financial phase in your life, while sharing experiences, both good and bad, from your previous stages with our younger personnel. This is YOUR idea, and what a terrific idea it is; we hope this new format aids you as requested.

Additionally, we have added a "True Cost of Coffee" analogy, extended our recommended website list based on your feedback, and enhanced our coverage for the Roth IRA and Home Mortgage sections. As requested, we kept the many analogies and comparisons in place that you enjoyed so much, especially the "Vince and Al" twin brother discussion on Survivor Benefit Plan and the "Free Money" discussion for post-military 401k retirement plans. We are thrilled with your feedback that this helps.

On the sad-but-true side, this version adds the 5 documents every military member should have in place (see page 1), when to update beneficiaries, and how to structure your beneficiary status if you have minor children (found on page 48). THIS IS ESPECIALLY IMPORTANT SO PLEASE SHARE THIS WITH YOUR FELLOW MILITARY HEROES!

While you liked the pocket-sized format of the original book, we've added 85 pages, so please provide feedback as to the new weight and thickness as well.

Material that YOU deemed unworthy has been excluded to make room for other topics you deemed more appropriate. If new pages aren't adding value, then they will be jettisoned in future updates. As always, it's up to you.

Please keep sending your comments and, as promised, we'll keep updating these pages to address YOUR concerns. As always, each of you is a hero; all Americans owe you a debt of gratitude, as we also owe to those who stood before you.

Very Respectfully,

Fred B. Strominger

GMEC Fred B. Strominger, USN (Ret)
Honorary Publisher, Joe Mann Books

TABLE OF CONTENTS

Preface   **Thanks For Your Feedback...**

SECTION 1 - DEPARTURE
Your First 5 Years of Military Service

Chapter 1   Driving a Car and the Fundamentals Of Money

Chapter 2   You Deserve To Pay Yourself

Chapter 3   Investment Debt versus Consumer Debt

Chapter 4   The TRUE Cost of a Purchase

Chapter 5   Start Your Roth IRA Now

Chapter 6   Important But Not-So-Pleasant Financial Decisions For Life

Chapter 7   Your Personal Financial Plan

SECTION 2 - MISSION
Re-enlistment Decisions
(Should I Stay or Should I Go?)

Chapter 8   Total Military Compensation

Chapter 9   Your Mortgage Matters

Chapter 10   How Do YOU Stack Up?

Chapter 11   Proven Techniques to KEEP You On Track For Your Goals

SECTION 3 - APPROACH
Pre-Retirement and Years 15-20+ of Military Service

Chapter 12   Military Pension Election Decisions
Chapter 13   Employment Benefits Decisions
Chapter 14   Real Estate, Income Taxes, and
              Unclaimed Property Searches

SECTION 4 - ARRIVAL
Post-Military Finances and Planning for
Your Survivor Spouse

Chapter 15   Post-Retirement Cashflow
              And Inflation
Chapter 16   Becoming More Financially
              Conservative in Retirement
Chapter 17   Contingency Planning As Your
              Final Act of Love

Appendix A – Real-World Financial Tales
Appendix B – The TRUE Cost of Coffee
Appendix C – The Daily Ledger
Appendix D – How Do **You** Stack Up?
Appendix E – Pro-Military Web Resources
              YOU Recommend Visiting
Index
Bibliography

This book belongs to you, the reader who enjoys it. Therefore, to add your comments, recommendations, or suggestions for future printings, please email them to the publisher at Discounts@ArmedForcesFunds.com

Section 1

DEPARTURE
Your First 5 Years of Military Service

Understand and apply these 7 habits NOW:
1. Spend less than you earn
2. Avoid consumption debt
3. Apply the Rule of 1/3 for future pay raises and bonuses
4. Utilize the IRS-style automatic savings method
5. Understand income tax preparation
6. Build your emergency fund
7. Contribute to a Roth IRA

Complete these 5 documents NOW:
1. Simple will
2. Power of Attorney for Finances
3. Power of Attorney for Healthcare
4. Emergency Data Sheet
5. POD titling for checking accounts

Read these 3 books from your local library:
1. The Richest Man in Babylon by George S. Clason
2. Get a Financial Life by Beth Kobliner
3. The Automatic Millionaire by David Bach

Chapter 1

Driving a Car and the Fundamentals of Money

Legendary football coach Vince Lombardi started every new season with the same words to his team: "We're going to start with the fundamentals. This is a football..." Who can argue with his success in football? Who can dispute his emphasis on the basics? Why don't we apply the same basic approach to your money?

Whether you are just joining the military, where you have a fresh new start on handling money, or have been active duty for a while, think of this as FINANCIAL SPRING TRAINING. From here let's touch on the fundamentals of money. **Handling your finances is like driving a car.** By now you've seen and ridden with countless drivers, whether your mode of transportation has been riding in a car, bus, train, rail, boat, or airplane. But did you REALLY PAY ATTENTION if you weren't driving? Probably not. Now that YOU are behind the wheel, driving is different, isn't it? Now that YOU are earning a paycheck every two weeks MONEY IS DIFFERENT, isn't it? You've been to driver's education class (and some perhaps to traffic school), but have you been to personal finance class?

In driver's ed you needed to know what different traffic signs meant. When did you have the right of way? When did you have to yield? How are green turn arrows

3

different than red turn arrows on stoplights? Before you took control behind the wheel you paid attention and heard experiences, both good and bad, from drivers who came before you. Your approach to money, your personal financial habits, will be much smoother if you take some time now and pay attention to the lessons and experiences of those veterans who walked in your moccasins long before you were born.

You will be getting paid twice per month for the entirety of your active duty career. **How much do you want to keep?** How much do you want to spend? **YOU** have the choice of when to spend, how much, and on what. Those are decisions **YOU** get to make.

When you first drove a car, YOU got to decide where you were going. YOU got to decide how to get there. If YOU had a final destination on a trip, YOU had control over what route to take to get there. Did you take the freeway to get there faster? Did you take side roads to enjoy the scenery? Whatever YOU decided, that's how you traveled the path. If your goal was to arrive in the shortest amount of time, would you pay attention to traffic jams that clogged certain highways? If there were expensive toll roads, would you take them? The same parallels apply to money management. There are proven routes to get you to your destination when driving.

There are also proven routes to get you to your financial goals. There are **traffic jams** (called excessive debt, consumer debt, and credit card debt) and **toll roads** (called expensive advice, automobile salesmen, and furniture salesmen) to watch out for on your journey. There are **freeways** (automatic savings and investments out of each paycheck) to get you there expeditiously. There are **side roads** (rental real estate, self-employment) that take a while but allow you to enjoy the journey. YOU get to decide how to get wherever YOU want to go. So first, let's talk about the fundamentals of money.

In the early days of mankind, each person secured her or his own food, water, and shelter. Some people had a knack for catching fish, but hated repairing their own shelter. Others found it a chore to hunt for food, but enjoyed building new huts. So the concept of trade was born – the fisherman could spend his time catching more fish, then trade what he couldn't eat to the builder, who in turn was helping build a hut for the fisherman. Each was happy.

A problem arose when the fisherman's hut was already built. How could the builder provide something of value to the fisherman in exchange for more fish? This is where the concept of money came into play. It is merely a medium to provide fair value for the exchange of goods and services. That's it. So eventually the fisherman and builder agreed upon an amount of money to trade for fish, allowing the fisherman to use this money for other goods and services he sought. And the concept of money, as used in trade, was born.

Bringing this concept forward to the 21st century, your employer (our government) offers you money for the goods and services you provide: manpower, skill, expertise, dedication, and defense of our country. YOU are empowered to spend this money on whatever YOU want. YOU get to decide how much to use NOW, for your current enjoyment, and how much to put away for later, for future enjoyment.

Looking back over the past 50 years, at the **millions** of veterans who have stood in YOUR place, just starting a military career, their collective feedback is to just put a little away out of every payday to have a small nest egg at the end of their career, however short or long that career may be. Of course, this same group has no regrets about money they spent on their unique worldwide travel, sightseeing, and souvenir sprees that are benefits of your special careers. They just wish they had spent slightly less, and put a little more money away for post-career lives.

If you want to **heed the advice** of your predecessors, the millions of military personnel who have gone before you, how to you follow their lead? Where do you begin? Let's begin by **thinking in terms of daily spending**. This is a common story, unfortunately, that showcases the unintended spending habits that can quickly get you off track from your desired approach to money.

If McDonald's charged $63 on its menu for a hamburger, would you buy one? Show of hands please? Then, how in the world could someone spend that much on one hamburger? Here's the story.

The legendary $63 hamburger story comes from experience, and it is an all-too-common tale. A 19-year old sailor stationed on Whidbey Island, WA went into McDonald's on base, paid for his McDLT meal (note to anyone under the age of 15 – this was a great meal that's no longer on the menu) with a personal check, and ate lunch. He thought (mistakenly, or this wouldn't be a story) he'd paid $3.00 for his meal. Instead, his check bounced. His bank put it through twice, charging his account $15 per try, and McDonald's charged $15 per try for a bounced, non-sufficient funds check. So all told, this individual paid $63 for his hamburger.

Now, this sailor certainly **didn't intend** to pay so much for his lunch, but it happened. It takes a lot of time and effort to correct a quick mishap like this, working with your bank and the merchant (in this case, a very cooperative and understanding McDonald's) to reverse the charges.

The entire situation could have been avoided had he ensured proper funds were available in his checking account. His lesson learned was simply to spend less than he earned. In the end, **he took responsibility** to ensure that he would never be overdrawn again. He **reviewed** his financial habits, didn't like what he saw, **stopped** doing what wasn't working, **started** doing what's been proven to work for others, and **changed his behavior** and, to this day, has kept his promise to himself.

Now this sailor wasn't 7-feet tall. He had average height, was a little overweight, had an average IQ, and an average attitude about life. There was nothing terribly special about him. He just realized that he needed to change his habits NOW to get where he was going. The path he was taking was not going to get him there in the timeframe he wanted. It wouldn't get him there at all. So wherever YOU are right now, is it where you WANT to be, or is it where you ENDED UP because you weren't yet paying full attention? YOU get to decide where you want to be. Just like this sailor, take a moment, decide WHERE you want to be, understand what habits you NEED to change to get there, and make those changes. It has been done in the past, it can also be done right now.

This $63 hamburger story has become a metaphor for **unintended spending** and a basic starting point to achieving financial goals. So, before you unintentionally start purchasing $63 hamburgers, let's **reassess** some of your financial choices and financial actions.

Action item #1 is for you to ask yourself if you are happy with your financial habits. What habits are working for you? Which habits are propelling you towards your financial goals? Which habits do you need to change? Which habits are detracting from your goals? This is our emphasis on the basics, our decision to go back to fundamentals. Once you **reinforce** your financial goals and **refocus** your decision-making process to achieve these goals, do you think you'll be better off or worse off? That choice is up to you – **whether you think you can or you think you can't, you're right.**

Chapter 2

You Deserve To Pay Yourself

Are you where you want to be financially? Why not start your new, solid, proven financial habits **RIGHT NOW?** What actions are you taking to reach your financial goals? What habits are you forming, **intentionally or by default**, to achieve your financial goals? It is said that the chains of habit are too light to be felt until they are too heavy to be broken. Think about that! Going back to fundamentals, if you start forming good financial habits now then they will continue for the rest of your life.

Whom have you chosen, intentionally or by default, to assist you in reaching your goals? You choose by the books you read and the people you meet. Have you read any good financial books lately? Have you spoken with others who financially are reaching their goals? Do you have a plan to get to your own goals? These are the questions to continually ask yourself as often as you'd like to keep you on a path to achieve your goals and to keep you motivated.

After all, NO ONE will watch your finances better than you. NO ONE will watch your money closer than you. NO ONE will watch your spending closer than you.

Are you looking for validation of your current financial habits? Do you seek other methods to achieve some financial stability in your life? Ever borrowed money between paychecks to buy food or gas? No matter what your current financial situation looks like, here are some

much-needed, time-tested tips to make your life easier and redirect you towards your financial goals.

And once you're back on your way, please share this knowledge with your family and friends to ensure smooth sailing for everyone. If your current money management style hasn't gotten you ahead, try a new tack. Listen to those who have come before you and save a portion of each paycheck. You vow to live on less than you earn. Now, how do you stop paying $63 for a hamburger?

You start by honestly answering this question: **Is your current spending pattern in line with your goals?** If not, then fix it. You don't have to wait for New Year's to make a resolution; just fix it RIGHT NOW.

If you just graduated from high school and are getting your first apartment, do you feel you immediately need a big-screen TV, VCR, DVD-player, couch, dining room table set, and new car? If the answer is yes, then you may want to think about these next paragraphs carefully.

If your habit is to **earn** $500 in one week, but you **spend** $550 on living expenses, then **how do you plan to get ahead?**

Look around you today at some of the individuals who have accumulated assets and you will find they have a very common thread. **These individuals live on less than they earn**. If they earn five hundred dollars in a week, they spend less than that, and save some of their earnings for the future.

There's a wise saying that states 'No business goes broke that makes a profit every day.' Let's extend this theory to individuals.

Here's an example of a young high school graduate, Kim, who's earning $1,600 each month. After withholding taxes and benefits payments she's left with just $1,380 monthly, which is $690 per paycheck received twice monthly.

Now, can she afford an $800 rent payment, a $275 car payment, $150 monthly auto insurance payment, $100 electric bill, $100 phone bill, new stereo, dine out 4 times per week, and still be putting money away for emergencies and for her future? Can she afford vet bills for animals, auto maintenance, and uniform upkeep?

If the social pressure to "keep up with the Joneses" is too great, Kim will find a way (think credit cards) to assimilate this lifestyle in the present **while robbing** her own future.

Every fixed income wage earner reaches a decision point of robbing future money accumulation to pay for current lifestyle. So let's ask again, *is your current spending pattern in line with your goals*?

What's a good remedy for Kim's all-too-common situation? One proven method, overwhelmingly, comes from the many veterans **who already lived this very lifestyle** while first starting out in life. Kim needs to **recognize her behavior**, namely spending more than she earns. She needs to recognize that **if she continues** this pattern, she will end up in tremendous debt at a young age, which will limit her options down the road. She is paying for her **current lifestyle** with **future earnings**.

Kim needs to RECOGNIZE her situation, often accompanied by bounced checks, low bank accounts, borrowing money from friends between paydays, and increasing credit card balances.

Once she **stops** doing the things that aren't working (spending more than she earns), and **starts** doing the proven things that work (spending less than she earns), she's on his way to achieving his financial goals.

Believe it or not, your predecessors who successfully set aside some money out of each paycheck even in the early, low-pay years, still managed to have great fun while in port or at home. They made use of discounted tickets for tours, events, and concerts through their military family centers. They enjoyed camaraderie through on-base sports centers, activity centers, and do-it-yourself automobile repair garages found on bases. Many would have PREFERRED to drive new cars, lounge on new furniture, and hold unlimited music and movie collections, but they recognized that on a limited income, these were not prudent long-term choices IF they were going to achieve financial goals.

It's tempting to buy the coolest sports car you can. It's tempting to buy the most fashionable clothes you can. If you're an E-3 driving a brand new Corvette, your peers may think you're cool. But most people will think, "How much does he owe every month on that car?" Your decisions now contribute to your habits, and these habits will be harder to break later in life. Spending and banking are habits you need to form now and reinforce periodically, making certain you are receiving full value for your decisions.

Referencing our $63 hamburger story, one of the biggest robbers of your income is **inefficient banking**. Overdraft fees, especially the dreaded Non-Sufficient Funds charges, and other associated fees can quickly spiral into the hundreds of dollars if your math is off unknowingly.

Banks collect these fees to offset the inconvenience of correcting overdrawn accounts and to provide a disincentive for you to do it again. So if you're caught in this trap, sit down with your local banker and find a way to remedy the situation. Don't be embarrassed – your banker will be more impressed that you desire to change, and may even waive some fees to encourage you on your way. They'll want to keep you as a satisfied customer with this attitude. If your banker doesn't, then find a new bank that will work with you towards your goals.

What other bank fees can you trim? How about your Automated Teller Machine (ATM) withdrawal habits? Do you withdraw $40 out of ATM when you're at your base exchange? How much is the fee if it ISN'T your bank's ATM? Is it a $1.50 charge? And how much does YOUR bank charge in addition to use a competitor's ATM? $1.00? So how much did it TRULY COST YOU to withdraw $40 from that ATM? If it cost $3.00 total in fees, then you've just paid 7.5 percent as a bank fee for the privilege of withdrawing your own money! Ouch!

How can you avoid this? Three simple solutions are apparent. First, join one of the banks or credit unions that have FREE ATM withdrawals at the locations where you ALREADY shop. This is especially important on overseas bases. Second, shop with a debit card to avoid paying ATM fees. Third, and most important, find a bank that REIMBURSES YOU for any ATM fees NOT in its network. Banks are responding to military member demands to reimburse up to $10 or more per month for ATM fees. This is a convenience to you, the consumer, for these banks NOT investing heavily into ATMs. You STILL have access to cash, and are reimbursed for a few ATM visits to other bank ATMs. THIS is the type of bank that works for you, TAKE TIME to seek out banks like this!

Here are **two other methods** to start turning around your spending and banking habits.

Each time you pay cash for a purchase of $10 or less, pay in dollars only. For instance, if you pay $3.49 for groceries, pay the cashier $4, then take the 51 cents in change and put it in a jar when you get home. If you continue this behavior, by the end of the month you'll be amazed at the amount of money that accumulates in your jar.

Also, after writing a check, record the check amount and round up by one dollar. If you write 12 checks each month, then you're already at least $12 ahead each month.

If money is really tight, then start by rounding up to the nearest dollar instead.

You'll find that you'll **always** have more in your checking account than you thought, and you'll never bounce a check again.

Once you get paid, does it seem like the money flows out of your checking account rather quickly? You pay rent to the landlord, an auto loan to a bank, credit card payments to a credit card company. You spend money for food at the commissary, make daily stops to convenience stores for coffee and donuts, and pay for uniforms, furniture, entertainment, and taxes.

But **do you pay yourself**? Do you pay yourself out of each paycheck? Do you realize that **a part of all you earn is yours to keep**? This mantra is repeated throughout a timeless financial book, *The Richest Man in Babylon,* by George S. Clason, which every high school and college-age student should read.

This concept is SO VITAL to your long-term finances in a capitalist society that it bears repeating. **A part of all you earn is yours to keep.** How does this apply to you?

Billy Bluejacket enlists in the Navy after graduating high school in June 2005. In his first 5 years of military service, entering as an E-1 and eventually rising to E-5, he can expect to earn approximately **$122,000!** That's how much will pass through his checkbook via direct deposit for his military pay, including allowances, in 5 years. Can you believe it? With limited skills and no experience, Billy is GETTING PAID to learn lifelong skills.

In sports terms, Billy has a 5-year, $122,000 contract.

How much will Billy keep?
That's entirely up to Billy!
How much will Billy pay to his landlord, his bank,

his fast food habits, his auto insurance company, etc.? Can Billy learn to pay himself FIRST, and then live on his remaining money? It's his choice. It's his money. But if he values the lessons learned from a plethora of veterans who have walked in his moccasins he will **LEARN TO** pay himself first so that he ALWAYS has financial choices in life. He will **form financial habits now**, based on fundamentals, to ensure his checkbook is never empty.

Saving money is a **choice**. It's YOUR choice. Did you ever think of it in these terms?

Here's another analogy that may turn around your thinking on the matter of paying yourself out of each paycheck.

Will you agree that the Internal Revenue Service is arguably the most successful debt collector in history? Have you noticed how the IRS collects income taxes? Do you think they wait until the end of the year, then send a bill to each wage earner? No way!

Each pay period, whether every week or every other week, they require wage payers to send in the collected dues out of each paycheck. Sure, you as a wage earner filled out your W-4 form to indicate how much they should take out, but still, every payday, there went your share owed to the IRS.

Now, what if you borrowed a page from their proven techniques, and **paid yourself** out of each paycheck? Do you think you'd be better or worse off in 5 years? Would you really miss that money? There's only one way to find out – try it and see.

This is the IRS-style automatic savings account concept. Just have an allotment set up from your direct deposit military paycheck each payday into any savings account. That's it. Have $25, $35, $50, or whatever YOU decide deposited **every payday**, and **do not touch it**. Let it pile up for a year. It's amazing that if you don't "see" that money in your checking account, you don't **spend** it. It's human nature. It's what makes the IRS tax collection technique so effective. **THIS IS EXACTLY WHAT YOUR PREDECESSORS, MILLIONS OF OTHER VETERANS WHO HAVE WALKED IN YOUR MOCCASINS, WANT YOU TO UNDERSTAND. JUST TRY IT!!!**

Once you decide on a financial goal, try implementing these proven strategies and you are on your way towards achieving it. Don't worry, as you age your goals will change. Your experiences, good and bad, will reinforce some of your lessons learned. The hardest part is getting started to save and invest, and staying motivated on your journey.

Action Item #2 is for you to decide whether or not you want to pay yourself. If so, then here's an easy way to start. Start an ALLOTMENT for $50 per PAYCHECK from your direct deposit pay right into your savings account. DO NOT TOUCH THIS MONEY for a few months! Take action NOW, set up this account, and form the habit of PAYING YOURSELF because you deserve it. It works for the IRS, it will work for you. As time goes on, **increase** this amount per paycheck, especially when you receive promotions and pay increases. Paying yourself first represents a fundamental cornerstone to achieving financial goals throughout your life.

Chapter 3

Investment Debt vs. Consumer Debt

There are two kinds of debt, investment debt and consumer debt. The difference between them is this: investment debt means financing an item that historically **appreciates** in value over time (think houses, coin collections, and stocks), while consumer debt is financing an item that historically **depreciates** in value over time (think automobiles, refrigerators, restaurant meals, computers, new clothing, stereos, DVDs, TIMESHARES, and compact disks).

A mortgage on your home represents investment debt. As you pay off your loan via installment (payments), the actual value of the home rises historically (for most homes). After a period of time, when the loan is paid off, you have a sizable, paid-for asset.

Credit card debt is the most common form of consumption debt. As you pay off your loan via installment (payments), the actual value of the consumed item is declining (or in the case of a meal, already consumed). Once your loan is paid off, you have **less than the original value** to show for it.

A common example of consumption debt is an automobile. If you finance a new automobile over a 5-year period and make payments every month, after 5 years (and 75,000 miles or so) is your auto worth more or less than when you bought it? **Much less of course!**

It's worth stopping here to mention timeshares. At some point each of you will qualify for a "free gift" for touring a timeshare property. Nothing in life is free. The underlying economics of TIMESHARES are NOT the same as will other real estate ownership. Please understand that going in. While some traits, such as tax deductible interest, are similar, timeshares RARELY increase in value over time. You cannot plan on selling your timeshare investment in 5 years for a profit.

Want more proof? Surf the internet for used timeshares and view the prices. By purchasing a timeshare, you are purchasing a vacation lifestyle. You are paying interest on loans, you are paying monthly "maintenance" fees, and you are purchasing an item that historically DEPRECIATES in value. If you tour one and decide to buy it, do so because you plan on vacationing in it. DO NOT buy it because "it's a good investment." As with ANY consumer purchase, buy it only if it fits your lifestyle and your budget. Only you can decide whether you will receive full value from your purchase, whether financial or emotional or both. It's your money. If you are counting on timeshare purchases to propel you towards short or long-term goals, then STOP and reevaluate, because historically THAT DOES NOT HAPPEN. Thank your friendly Coast Guard veteran Mike for highlighting this area of misunderstanding.

Another example is renting versus buying a home. Are you paying high rent every month to live in a "luxury" apartment? Why not buy a home with roughly the same mortgage payment as your rent, even though it may not be a "luxury" home? Remember the time-tested truism that states: Paying rent secures another's financial future, but paying your own mortgage secures your own.

So let's **look at your spending behavior** and encourage buying appreciating items with your money.

If you're buying a car, consider buying a less expensive, almost new, lower cost automobile. If your goal is reliable transportation, isn't this a viable solution? While you know you need transportation, you will pay less for a 2-year old car, typically have lower insurance costs, and perhaps even lower finance costs.

If you will deploy soon, can you delay your purchase until you return? **Does it make sense** to buy a car now, knowing it will sit in the driveway until you return in 8 months?

After speaking with **thousands of prior veterans**, a common thread emerges. One group became aware of consumption debt at a young age and limited the amount of automobiles they purchased throughout their careers. They typically held onto cars longer, paid much lower insurance rates through the years, and paid less on auto loans because they saved up to make larger down payments on their next auto. The other group continued buying new cars every few years, paid higher insurance costs, paid more on average in financing for their lifestyle choice, and retired with considerably less assets than those who bought used cars.

These veterans disclosed another gem to pass along to you. Across the board, they were EXCELLENT at saving money while deployed! During deployments, veterans spent little or none of their paychecks. Their money piled up in checking accounts. However, almost to a person, they **BOUGHT HIGH-COST CONSUMER ITEMS** upon their return from deployment! Many purchased automobiles, typically putting a large downpayment on a car they'd REALLY wanted. Others purchased top-shelf stereos, computers, clothing, furniture, and CDs. VERY FEW admitted they paid down debt of ANY type, including credit card debt built up from previous overspending on consumer items. Only 3 fully funded IRAs with their forced savings (note that the Thrift Savings Plan was not available prior to 2002 for military personnel.)

Don't take their experiences the wrong way. This is not to say that it isn't terrific to own a new car. This is stating that YOU have choices to make, and that exchanging **current cars** for **new cars** every few years **depletes your cash** from other areas and other financial goals. Simply put, on a fixed salary, there is only so much money to be spent per month, and when auto payments, insurance, and auto operating costs take a significant percentage of your income, you may want to be sure that's your intention.

If you're NOT receiving full value and full enjoyment from the amount you spend monthly on your car, then rethink your approach to automobiles. Historically speaking, plenty of veterans would go back in time and **change their spending**, so let's pass their experiences on to you, and let you decide for yourselves. Either way, you are informed of the amount of money historically spent on autos, so whatever choice you make, just make sure you're getting enjoyment from your choice.

Besides automobiles, dinners in fast-food restaurants represent the other typical overspending. What is the cost of a dinner out? Is it $20? That depends on your tastes. If you and your spouse worked all week, and decided to eat at a restaurant Friday evening, how much would you spend? Would you order appetizers, adult beverages, and desserts? How about ordering a fancy seafood dish, or an expensive bottle of champagne? How much do you tip? 12%? 15%? 25%? Again, this depends on your tastes and preferences.

Two of the best dining out tips around are as follows: Remember that waiters, waitresses, and bartenders all depend on tips for their rent, transportation, and living expenses. If they provide good service, including recommendations off the menu, please tip accordingly. It takes just as much effort to keep bringing you fresh water as it does to bring you a soda. If you can afford to pay $18 for a steak dinner that you could cook for $4 at home, then don't forget to factor in a tip for the service provided.

Secondly, if you're going to eat out, why not order something you wouldn't cook for yourself? Do you make an awesome linguine with clam sauce? Then why order it out? Do you grill the meanest steak in your neighborhood? Then why order one when you eat out? To help make the occasion special, try something new that you wouldn't cook for yourself. Then see if your dining dollars don't seem better spent.

Action Item #3 is to evaluate how much consumer debt you are paying and how much investment debt you are paying. If you are paying consumer debt, whether it is to credit card companies or a consolidation loan, decide whether this is a habit you want to keep. If not, then commit to changing course. STOP the actions, namely spending on consumer items, which contributed to consumer debt, and START the actions that will keep you on your path to your financial goals. After all, YOU decide how much of your earnings YOU want to keep based on your financial decisions.

Chapter 4

The TRUE Cost of a Purchase

Let's say you are window shopping and you see a pair of sunglasses you've just got to have. The price tag reads $50, marked down from $100. Now here's the tricky question: **how much will it cost you to buy those sunglasses?**

If you answered $50 plus sales tax, congratulations! So you actually got to the counter and it cost you $53.50, after the sales tax was included. Is that your final answer, $53.50? Then how about this – **how much did you have to earn in your paycheck to spend $53.50 after taxes?** If you're in the 28% marginal tax bracket, then you actually had to earn $68.48 to pay $53.50 after taxes to buy these sunglasses. If you earn $14 per hour at your work, then you **had to work 4.9 hours** to buy these sunglasses.

So now, the **cost** of our new purchase **has risen from $50 to $68.48** when we really think it through. **Is it still worth it?** Was it worth working 4.9 hours just to pay for those sunglasses? Only you can decide. Just be aware what the true cost is, and decide if you're receiving **your full value** for your hard-earned money!

While the TRUE cost of sunglasses may raise your eyebrows, what if we applied this concept to cars? If you are in the 15% income tax bracket, and sales tax is 8%, how much does a $20,000 car really cost? Sales tax is $1,600, so your car now costs $21,600. You need to earn $24,840 to pay $21,600 after tax for this purchase. Does THAT raise your eyebrows? There is some unintended overspending in this $20,000 automobile purchase, isn't there?

Dining out, paying for cell phones, and purchasing clothing items "on sale" represent three of the most common forms of **unintended overspending**. This is simply impulse purchasing justified with "but it was on sale."

Please, for the sake of your financial goals, remember to think about how much you intend to spend *prior to making your decision* to dine out, upgrade your cell plan, or shop. By getting full value for your dollars they'll stretch further than you think!

Is it necessary to control your unintended overspending? Of course! What good mariner can sail without taking into effect the currents and wind? What solid financial plan does not account for unintended spending? First, a handy analogy for what we are about to embark on.

When was the last time you flew in an airplane? Think about this analogy. If you're departing from Las Vegas, NV and heading for San Antonio, TX, how would you plan your flight? Would you head due north? Probably not, as San Antonio is southeast of Las Vegas.

So you'd take off, head the plane southeast, and relax, right? That sounds good so far. There's just one flaw in this plan: you are not taking into account the effects that the wind can have on you. See, you can have the perfect heading after you take off from Las Vegas that, according to a chart, or map, will have you in San Antonio in exactly 3 hours. But after a little while the wind probably blows you off course. Do you NEED TO redirect the plane straight for San Antonio again?

Well, that would help, certainly. **You need to change course**, no doubt, because if you remain on your original heading you won't ever arrive if the conditions don't change. But, if you redirect the plane directly towards San Antonio, then after a while the winds will still blow you off course.

What you really need to do is correct for the wind by taking into account its effects on your efforts. **Anticipate its effects**, and crab into the wind appropriately to counter its effects. This will provide you with a more accurate path toward your goal.

And guess what? You'll still need to **check your progress periodically**, to see if the wind is blowing you off course, or the wind has shifted, or your speed has slowed. So it's a matter of finding out where you are, defining your goal, monitoring your progress to this point, **correcting your efforts as necessary**, and redirecting your efforts to more efficiently achieve your goal.

Hey, this is beginning to make sense, right? The same is true for your financial goals. The same basic game plan still holds.

Just because **you're not EXACTLY** where you want to be right now doesn't mean you can't get there. Be honest with yourself – what was your goal, what behavior led to your getting off course, and what will you do to correct it?

Action Item #4 is to identify how much you REALLY paid for your last 3 big purchases. Typically this includes a car, a stereo, and a cell phone. For example, if you bought a $250 stereo, how much sales tax did you pay? Assuming you are in the 15% federal income tax bracket, take the entire amount, purchase plus sales tax, and multiply by 1.15. This will give you a rough estimate of how much you need to earn to pay for this after tax. Did you pay for this on a credit card? If so, what interest rate does it charge? How long will you pay on this purchase until it is paid off? Add in the interest to find out how much you really paid for this item. Only YOU know if that was money well spent.

Chapter 5

Start Your Roth IRA Now

Although medicines protect you and prevent diseases, they don't often taste good. There are parallels in financial planning for the medicines that protect us and keep us healthy. These medicines are called emergency savings, life insurance, disability insurance, health insurance, auto insurance, homeowners insurance, renters insurance, wills, powers of attorney, and emergency data sheets. Let's touch on the importance of each as well as common techniques for you to ponder.

If you view your emergency savings account as your pants pocket, then let's put money in and continuously "leave it overnight." Don't touch it. Don't spend it. Let it accumulate. It feels good. It looks good. Most of all it provides the confidence to move to the next step, investing.

Once you have proven to yourself that you are disciplined enough to save money from each paycheck, then gradually branch out and redirect money monthly to fund your short and long-term goals. If short-term goals are within a year, then STRONGLY consider using a fixed principle account, such as a savings account or money market, to save your money. Your principal will not fluctuate, and interest will accumulate. Best of all, it is federally insured by the Federal Deposit Insurance Corporation (FDIC). Find the highest-paying interest account that allows you to grow the most money without any type of penalty for early withdrawal.

For your longer term goals, consider investments. Go to your library and check out a book about stocks, bonds, and mutual funds. These can be wonderful vehicles to fund your long term objectives, including retirement and education. In fact, our government is so highly interested in educating YOU to invest for your OWN retirement that there are special, tax-preferred accounts in which you can avoid taxes during your earning years IF you want to turbo-charge your retirement account. **TAKE ADVANTAGE OF THESE!**

When our government offers tax rebates or tax incentives to encourage behavior, **take advantage of it!** Our government is driving behavior with tax incentives. The easiest two examples to cite are home ownership (mortgage interest is tax deductible) and education (school loans are tax deductible). For retirement, our government allows the income you put away in a specified retirement account to avoid current taxes (think of your Thrift Savings Plan, or TSP), or pay tax now and NEVER PAY INCOME TAX AGAIN (think Roth IRA). Best of all, if you have adjusted gross income below $25,000, they offer a **Retirement Savings Contribution Credit** to reward you for savings towards your own retirement! It's often overlooked, but found in IRS Publication 590, claimed on Form 8880, and your credit back, **only on contributions up to $2,000 in 2005**, can range from 10% to 50%!

Taken in context, if the government is providing a generous tax break just because you are contributing to your own retirement, it acts similar to an employer match for a Roth IRA or a Thrift Savings Plan contribution. It isn't identical because the match is not provided inside of your retirement plan. But if you contribute to your Roth IRA, the government DECREASES your income tax burden when you claim your contribution on form 8880, so you will pay less in income taxes or get a larger refund because of your investment behavior. ISN'T THAT FANTASTIC?

Let's look at this in another light. If you are an E-3 in any branch of service, single, and have no other income, and if you automatically contribute **just $167** (or $333 to maximize your annual contribution) per month into a Roth IRA as recommended starting in January, your government is going to LOWER your income taxes due by an extra **$1,000** next year. Want another great analogy? If your goal is to save $1,000 for a big-screen TV next year, but you still want to contribute to your retirement savings as you know you should, then just contribute **$167 monthly** and next year the government will BUY YOU YOUR BIG SCREEN TV! If THAT isn't incentive to invest for your future retirement, nothing is. **DO IT!**

Another common question asked is whether or not to invest in the Thrift Savings Plan (TSP) or a Roth IRA. Remember, the military TSP does NOT offer a match for most participants, and is a pre-tax retirement funded vehicle (it is not included as taxable income now; you will pay income tax in retirement when you withdraw funds from this account). A Roth IRA is an after-tax retirement vehicle, meaning you WILL pay tax on the earned income you fund it with, contribute to your Roth IRA, it will grow tax deferred, and you WILL NOT pay any tax in retirement when you withdraw from this account.

Having framed the debate, here is the gouge.

IF you qualify for special incentive pay that entitles you to receive a match on your military TSP contribution, then contribute up to the percentage that will be matched.

IF you will NOT receive any matching contribution for your TSP, then base your contribution on your current tax situation. If you are in a LOW tax bracket now (15%), contribute to a Roth IRA. If you are in a medium tax bracket (25%) or higher, and anticipate being in a LOWER tax bracket in retirement, then contribute to your TSP first. If you are in a medium tax bracket (25%) or higher, and anticipate being in a HIGHER tax bracket in retirement, then contribute to a Roth IRA first up to the maximum limit, and then contribute to your TSP.

IF you think you might need a lump sum of money to start a business, fund education, or purchase a home in 6 or more years, then fund a Roth IRA. Please read on for the reasoning behind these general guidelines. As always, ask for a second opinion for how this applies to you, as this could keep thousands of dollars in YOUR POCKET down the road if you take advantage of tax laws now.

IF you will receive ANY type of matching funds for your TSP contribution, then fund up to that amount. For instance, if you qualify as a military member for a special program where your incentive pay, bonus, or special pay will be matched by the government up to a certain percentage, then this truly is a wonderful way to finance your retirement, and it is STRONGLY recommended you contribute up to that percentage into your TSP. This is FREE MONEY to you, so take advantage of it. This **MAY PLAY** a significant factor with new operational bonuses for all special forces personnel of all service branches. For example, if the government offers a special 20% match on up to $30,000 bonus money you invest in the TSP, and your goal is to contribute to a secure retirement fund, then by contributing $30,000 the government adds $6,000. You've just guaranteed yourself a 20% return on your investment with **NO RISK!** It will continue working for you into the future. This will turbo-charge your retirement investments going forward, and is a terrific habit to retain.

IF you will NOT receive any matching, then consider this. If you are already earning less than $30,000/yr for single tax filers (or $60,000 for married filers) of

TAXABLE income, contribute to a Roth IRA. You will be funding your retirement with after-tax dollars now, but your money will grow tax-deferred, and when you take money out in retirement it will be tax FREE to you. So you will have paid 15% tax on your contribution, but the earnings will never be taxed! If you are an E-5 or below and single, consider funding your retirement with a Roth IRA contribution rather than a TSP contribution.

HEED THIS ADVICE! Your predecessors brought up a solid point. If you retire with a military pension, you are 92% certain of being in the 25% federal tax bracket or higher when you fully retire. By receiving military pension and Social Security, your annual pension cash flow puts you in this bracket. Any money you remove from other retirement accounts, including TSP, will be taxed as ORDINARY INCOME to you, meaning when you remove $1 you will pay at least 25 cents in federal taxes. **THIS IS WHY THEY STRONGLY RECOMMEND FUNDING YOUR ROTH IRA FIRST!**

Let's take the case of twin siblings Allan Retirement and his sister Roni Retirement. Both are 22 year-old E-5s in the Coast Guard, both are single, and both are considering saving more money for long-term goals. Allan is a Coast Guard lifer, but Roni isn't sure this is the career for her, and may get out after her enlistment ends in 5 years. Both are in the **15%** federal income tax bracket with their E-5 earnings.

Allan begins investing $100 per month in the TSP. Since he is funding his TSP with pre-tax dollars, this in effect means he avoids $15 per contribution in federal income taxes. If he contributes for 5 years, his total contributions are $6,000. He has also saved $900 in income taxes due to the pre-tax feature of his TSP contributions. His money grows at 9% on average, and when he is 60 years old it will have grown to $175,000!! However, as he takes this money out, he is now in a higher tax bracket,

25%, due to his Coast Guard retirement pay, so when he withdraws $10,000, he must pay $2,500 federal income tax on this money. His $175,000 is really, $131,000 of spending after taxes.

Roni, on the other hand, duplicates brother Allan's contribution but chooses a Roth IRA for her investment. She also funds $100 per month for just 5 years, but hers is an after-tax contribution, so she does pays additional taxes of **15%**, or $180 each year, that Allan does not pay yet. Her money also grows at 9% and when she is 60 years old her account totals $175,000 as well. However, since she paid into the Roth IRA with after-tax dollars, she pays **NO INCOME TAXES** on ANY of her Roth IRA value when she withdraws it! She paid tax at the 15% bracket originally, but pays NO TAXES now regardless of her future income tax bracket. That is the benefit of the Roth IRA. She has $175,000 of money to spend!!!!

While Allan chose to take his tax deduction now by contributing to his TSP, Roni chose to pay her tax now while she was in a low income tax bracket in exchange for tax-free withdrawals in retirement. Most importantly, she had **one additional advantage: FLEXIBILITY!** Had she needed the money in 5 years to transition from the military back to civilian life, she could have withdrawn ALL of her contributions with no penalty and no tax consequence. This **flexibility**, offered to qualified Roth IRA contributors, makes a Roth IRA the preferred funding vehicle for young and low-current-tax bracket military members.

A Roth IRA is the most **UNDER-UTILIZED and consequently UNDER-APPRECIATED** savings method for young sailors, airmen and soldiers today, bar none. (**Publisher's note**: Our special thanks to Petty Officer Russ Adsit, USN (Ret), for his multiple efforts to hammer this point home to our young troops via his feedback from the first book.)

What is a recommended method to fund a Roth IRA? Invest in mutual funds. This is the strongest recommendation by other veterans. Since your primary job is to become an expert in your military field, why not delegate the day-to-day financial decisions to a mutual fund manager to oversee your investments? A solid **no-load** mutual fund, with low minimum investments, funded with monthly allotments straight from your military paycheck is a proven method to get started.

Specifically, since you are young, have a long time horizon to investment, and plan on using this mainly for retirement, consider using one of the following successful mutual funds for your initial Roth IRA investment. These funds and fund families were mentioned in feedback from members and are highlighted in Beth Kobliner's 1996 release, "Get A Financial Life," that many of you enjoyed. Since almost 10 years have passed since the release of her book, the results are coming in...and they are positive. You liked her ideas, you followed her advice, and you are financially more aware and stronger today because of her material. Here then are your recommended funds:

1. American Century Capital Value Fund
   1-877-44-AMCEN
   www.americancentury.com
2. Fidelity Low-Priced Stock Fund
   1-800-FIDELITY
   www.fidelity.com
3. T. Rowe Price Capital Appreciation Fund
   1-866-436-1393
   www.troweprice.com
4. USAA Extended Market Index Fund
   1-800-472-8722
   www.usaa.com

Just call, speak with a licensed representative at any of the above companies, and they will be more than willing to send you a prospectus, help you fill out paperwork, and get started on this crucial initial step. From time to time each company may make certain mutual funds unavailable, but they will always make a solid recommendation suited to your timeframes and investment goals. Take this for action and welcome to the world of investing!

Some of the feedback centers on index funds versus managed funds and load mutual funds versus no-load funds. A few of you inquired about Exchange Traded Funds (ETF) and contractual plans. Many of you are already investing monthly in variable annuities and equity income annuities. Some expressed their joy at investing for college and retirement in a whole life insurance plan and a variable universal life insurance policy. Let's briefly touch on each of these based on **why the previous four no-load mutual funds** (or similar no-load replacements) were singled out by your peers and veterans as being investor-friendly when starting your initial allotments.

Mutual funds are offered in two types, managed funds and index funds. Managed funds have active managers (or teams) responsible for daily investment selection towards the fund's goal. On the plus side, it's like having a pilot in an airplane to make critical timely decisions. On the down side, it costs money to pay these skilled managers so it adds costs to the annual expenses to run these funds. The first 3 funds mentioned, from American Century, Fidelity, and T. Rowe Price, are all no-load managed funds.

Index funds by design simply mirror the underlying index, most common of which is the Standard and Poor's 500 index, which tracks the largest 500 companies trading on the New York Stock Exchange. These funds do not have a specific manager, but simply buy and sell based on movements in the indices. They are tax efficient, have small annual expenses so you keep more of your gains, and have become prevalent in retirement plans in the last ten years. The last fund, USAA, is an index fund recommended by others who have been in your shoes.

Load mutual funds charge sales fees to enter, exit, or both. These sales charges reduce overall performance by increasing costs. If your fund indicates "A" shares, you paid a front-end sales charge. If it indicates "B" shares, you will pay a back end sales fee if redeemed within a certain number of years. If you own "C" shares, you are paying a significantly higher annual charge to pay your advisor who sold you the fund. While these high sales charges, whether A, B, or C shares, are great for the advisor's salary, they are NOT so great for your investment returns. Historical evidence indicates no significant evidence that load mutual funds outperform no-load mutual funds, so this is why none of the four above-mentioned recommendations from your peers is a load fund. **Consider following the advice** of those who came before you, and start investing automatically, via allotment, in a proper no-load mutual fund. If you are doing your own research, then you **deserve** to keep more money in your pocket!

Contractual plans represent another form of load mutual funds, as many of you commented. These are commonly sold to young investors new to the investment arena. These plans are high in sales fees, but in fairness the financial sales force needs to be paid somehow for their efforts in explaining how they work and keeping investors informed. Historically from your feedback, years later, when members find out that they paid 50% commissions during the first year they invested in various investments, they are actually angry at the outrageous price. But the bottom line is they SAVED AND INVESTED MONEY along the way that they otherwise would not have saved.

Just like booster rockets during the initial stages of launch, load mutual funds and contractual plans provide tremendous energy to change your financial habits. It took the financial salesman a lot of explaining, training, and paperwork follow-up to start your accounts. You have saved money, which was your goal, accumulated assets, and increased your net worth. At some point though, your booster rockets have **served their purpose** – consider **jettisoning** them at this stage. Once you remain confident by understanding the fundamentals of investing towards your goals, why not move to less expensive investment techniques, such as no-load mutual funds, to propel you towards your goals more efficiently?

No-load mutual funds do not charge sales fees for purchases or redemptions. That is why they may not always be offered for sale or recommended by your local financial advisors. If you look around you can find all kinds of information on no-load funds offered directly from the fund families themselves. On the plus side, you typically pay much lower annual expenses when owning these funds. On the down side, you need to take initiative to call the companies that offer them to buy them, but they typically have outstanding phone and internet support regarding assistance to you, the investor.

ETFs are becoming a hot topic among mutual fund investors. They are currently index funds that trade during the day much like a stock. There are no managed ETFs at this time, although there is discussion about managed ETFs in the future. Barclay's dominates the current ETF market. They offer low internal annual costs and minimal transaction fees. However, if you dollar cost average LESS THAN $2,000 **per month**, then this can be a **very expensive** method to fund your Roth IRA, as there are transaction fees for **each purchase** or redemption. For ETFs to help you right now, wait until you have built a nice sum of money, and THEN consider moving it to an ETF. Until then, DO NOT dollar-cost average monthly into an ETF or the transaction costs will degrade your return significantly. Use a no-load mutual fund until then.

Annuity sales have come under strict scrutiny of late also, the main complaint centering on how they are misrepresented by agents who earn high commissions on their sales. Remember that all annuities are insurance contracts, meaning there is an insurance component that adds cost, and usually a higher administrative fee as well. THIS PRECLUDES VARIABLE ANNUITIES FROM BEING FUNDAMENTALLY EFFICIENT INVESTMENT VEHICLES. This represents an automatic added expense that detracts from your financial goals, be they short or long term. Equity index annuities (EIA) share the same drawbacks, namely higher expenses and insurance costs passed along to you, whether you want them or not.

Neither EIAs or variable annuities represent the best pure investment selections for your initial investments towards financial goals. These insurance products cannot be honestly sold as the most efficient means to accumulate money towards any primary financial goal. They DO have a place in the investment world, just as in football terms a deep-threat wide receiver has a place in any offense, but no team throws to the same receiver on every play.

You are probably better off passing on these types of insurance products until you've accumulated significant investments, your risk tolerance decreases, and you want to protect against market risk. Then there's a place for either of these products for a portion of your portfolio to diversify across investments by integrating insurance into your overall portfolio. If a salesman pushes you hard (these are sold, they are not bought) to buy these as a primary investment goal, just say no thank you, and reference this passage. There are ongoing investigations by state insurance agencies, SEC, and NASD regarding inappropriate insurance product sales. Avoid them as your primary investment vehicle. That's the advice passed along from MANY of your predecessors via their e-mails.

Should you use whole life insurance policies, universal life insurance, and variable life insurance policies as primary investment vehicles for college education, retirement, or short-term goals? DON'T DO IT. Once again, for the same reasons as previously mentioned with variable annuities and EIAs, added insurance costs and expenses severely inhibit investment performance. These ARE NOT primary investment vehicles! If you have an insurance need, and want to BLEND that need with some forced savings and investments, then these products may be appropriate. There are income tax incentives and consequences for these types of investments, so tread carefully, being sure that you need the insurance coverage prior to purchasing a policy based solely on "investment" needs.

Your predecessors overwhelmingly lean towards no-load mutual funds as primary investment vehicles for financial goals. If you are still undecided, review this chapter again before proceeding to the next action item.

Action Items #5 is to kick-start your flexible-term investing by picking up the telephone and calling one of the no-load mutual fund companies listed on page 33. Enhance your conversation by stating you are interested in starting a monthly Roth IRA allotment and you want some help setting it up. Any of these companies can help you get started, typically with $50 per month or less commitments. If the minimums are higher, simply thank them and call one of the other companies listed. It's YOUR money, not theirs, so YOU decide how much per month to invest!

Chapter 6

Important But Not-So-Pleasant Financial Decisions For Life

Now that you are taking action towards achieving your financial goals by funding a Roth IRA, it's time to touch on the "what if?" questions. First, what if you die? Do you REALLY need a will if you're 18 years old, an E-2 in the Army, and your belongings include a lot of new uniforms and a stereo? The answer is a loud, emphatic YES! EVERYONE needs a will (or a will substitute). If you don't take time to draw out a will, your state government has one for you, and you may not like them deciding how your assets are divided and to whom. So take some time and effort now, get a will in place, and update it periodically as you acquire assets and move throughout your military career.

Of course, any discussion of a complicated subject such as a last will and testament, part of overall estate planning, deserves a disclaimer – so please review appropriate information carefully before creating a will.

Ironically, estate planning isn't just for the wealthy. It is for everyone. Estate planning is simply **accountability** for your heirs. Everyone will eventually die; we just don't know exactly when. So each of us should take accountability to ensure we have addressed the issue of where we want our assets, however small or large they may be, to be distributed after we die.

The simple truth to the matter is this: we all have a death contingency plan for our belongings. If YOU want to decide where your property goes, then write a will. If you HAVEN'T written a will, then each state has a will for you, called intestate succession laws. The state will then decide, via court hearings, where your assets go and how they are to be distributed if you have not taken time to write a will on your own.

So, simply put, who do YOU think knows better where YOU want YOUR belongings to go, YOU or the state? Please take time, visit your local Judge Advocate General office, and have at least a simple will drawn up for yourself (and your spouse, if married).

Many veterans wrote in that their local JAG office was too busy to expediently draw up a simple will, while others wrote that they were die-hard do-it-yourself type personalities. They countered that there is sufficient information online and at their local libraries to draw up their own simple wills. You may wish to consider buying a do-it-yourself will kit (or software) at a local business store. Here are a few websites worth mentioning from your feedback, each company received satisfactory approval from veterans:

1. www.nolo.com
2. www.planmywill.com
3. www.wills-net.com
4. www.willsondemand.com

Consider visiting any of the above sites online for additional guidance on writing your own simple will. Also, consider visiting your local library, a local Barnes & Noble or www.bn.com for a copy of a superior book on estate planning, written by Michael T. Palermo, titled *AARP Crash Course in Estate Planning.* This book is supported and recommended by the American Association of Retired Persons (AARP). Your feedback overwhelmingly suggests these references were superior to any other on the market.

Every time you change duty stations between states you **need to update** your will for the new state. Remember that the intestate succession laws vary by state, and are not national in nature, so it is **vital** to ensure you keep your wills updated as you change residences between states. As a quick example, let's take the based-on-a-true-story situation of twin sisters Carey and Claire. (For you readers from the previous version, they are not related to Al and Vince). Both are 20 years old, own a $5,000 car, have $5,000 in mutual funds, a $7,000 Roth IRA account, and have $2,000 in a checking account. Both are stationed in Virginia Beach, VA, and both attend a command brief that reminds them to update their wills for their new duty station. Carey and Claire decide to leave all possessions to their fiancés, Mike and Mick.

Carey makes an appointment at her local Judge Advocate General office to create a thorough, detailed will, and Claire locates a cheap online do-it-yourself will website, paying $79 to input her information and print out a valid will. Carey spends two hours filling out a standard pre-will worksheet, detailing every possession, and makes an appointment two weeks out to meet with a JAG attorney to review and sign her will. Claire fills out a 10-minute online questionnaire, prints out her simple will document, drives to a nearby notary at her local United Parcel Service (UPS) counter (banks don't notarize for free anymore), and signs her simple will in front of two witnesses, then notarizes her document. Later that night, tragically, both Carey and Claire are killed in an unexpected boating accident. Did they each achieve their desired accountability for their assets after their unexpected deaths? **No!**

Carey's will is NOT valid, as it has not been signed and witnessed. Although she took time and effort to make a detailed will, it will not be recognized by the probate court in Virginia. Carey therefore died intestate, meaning without

41

a valid will. The state of Virginia, through its intestate laws, now decides that one-half of Carey's estate goes to her parents, and one-half to her surviving sisters Danielle and Veronica. Her fiancé, Mike, gets absolutely nothing. Her church gets absolutely nothing. This is a sad but too-often-true story of unintended consequences.

Although Claire signed a simple, inexpensive will, **it is valid** and will be recognized by the state of Virginia probate court. With estates under $1 million, it is **extremely rare to have a will challenged in court**, regardless of the state court presiding. Since Claire's will was properly signed and witnessed, her wishes will be followed and her fiancé Mick will be the recipient of all assets passing through probate.

This example with Carey and Claire by no means diminishes the professional wills drawn up for free through your local JAG office. Rather, it is meant to highlight the importance that a signed, valid simple will, especially for young personnel with minimal assets, is better than no signed will at all (even a free one).

Please note for each of these sisters that their Roth IRAs will pass outside of probate. Retirement plans offer account owners a beneficiary designation in the event of death, similar to life insurance policies. Both Carey and Claire would have filled out their Roth IRA beneficiary designation forms and, upon their tragic deaths, these assets would have passed to their desired heirs, namely Mike and Mick, outside of the probate and intestate law processes. So this serves also as a reminder to **update your beneficiaries** for all retirement plans and insurance policies on a periodic basis also to ensure they reflect your wishes in the event of an untimely demise.

While a will provides accountability if you die, what happens if you live but are incapacitated? Who makes decisions for you then? YOU need to decide that right now, paralleling your decisions when you made out a will.

Take time and draw up two other important documents when you have your will drawn up. These documents are a Durable Power of Attorney for Healthcare and a Durable Power of Attorney for Finances. This enables YOU to decide, in writing, WHO will make healthcare decisions for you if you are incapacitated, and WHO will make financial decisions on your behalf. These two documents, like your will, provide accountability and direction from you and, when needed, provide an enormous relief to your loved ones that they are following your wishes by following your directives. Think of the second-guessing you eliminate by providing clear directions to your loved ones under these conditions.

Just as with wills, powers of attorney need to be periodically reviewed and updated, especially when you change duty stations and move to another state. Make a commitment to incorporate these documents into your annual financial review as the years go by.

As long as we're discussing death and disability in the context of wills and Powers of Attorney, we may as well touch on life insurance and disability insurance. As with all forms of insurance, there are three approaches you can take. You can RETAIN the risk, you can SHIFT the risk, or you can SHARE the risk. This drives the fundamentals of all insurance discussions.

You have a wonderful, flexible coverage available called Servicemen's Group Life Insurance, or SGLI, that is extremely cheap for the amounts of coverage. There is no 'War Clause', meaning if you die during wartime conditions it still pays out to your beneficiaries. BEWARE of life insurance policies that DO NOT contain this war clause. Those policies will NOT fully cover you as desired if you die during war conditions!

In your feedback you identified a wonderful source to compare life insurance quotes. You visited reliaquote.com online, answered some brief questions, and received multiple quotes for term insurance policies. BE CAREFUL regarding these policies because some DO NOT contain War Clauses! What good does it serve to identify, qualify, and purchase a term life policy IF IT DOES NOT SERVE YOUR MAIN PURPOSE, which includes your untimely death during war conditions? Find a policy that DOES include a war clause, then compare it to a policy from one of the military organizations that sells life insurance, as all contain a war clause. These include **USAA, AFBA, and Armed Forces Insurance**. That is a more fair comparison, and better serves your purpose in paying those premiums in the first place. Our special thanks extend to Joe in Maryland for this tidbit.

Do you NEED life insurance? Let's first frame the purpose of life insurance. IF YOU HAVE a spouse, children, parent, or anyone DEPENDENT on YOUR FINANCIAL EARNED INCOME, there is a need for life insurance. For example, if you have a $25,000 annual salary, then in the next 10 years, with no bonuses and no pay increases, you will expect to have $250,000 flow through your checking account. You can reasonably expect to use this income to pay on a mortgage, pay off education loans, pay for an automobile, provide for your spouse, children, parents, neighbors, pets, etc. But if you die, this income stream is shut off. No income will flow through your checking account, and thus your dependents will NOT have your financial support for them to continue living at their current means. This, in a nutshell, is why Life Insurance is sometimes called an act of love.

By using a portion of your earnings to pay for life insurance premiums, you are essentially saying to those dependent on you "If I die, I still want to provide for a portion of your financial dreams." Translation: if you die, here's a chunk of money to pay off the mortgage so you don't have to move, pay off any other debts, and provide a few years of living expenses to provide time for the surviving spouse to return to work, improve on education, or adapt to the loss of you.

Life insurance is fundamentally a bet between you and your life insurance company that you are going to die. Your SGLI is a form of term life insurance, a pure type life insurance at this stage in your career. Simply put, you pay the insurance company a premium each month betting that you are going to die. If you die, they lose, and must pay your designated beneficiaries (that you select) the amount of insurance. If you DON'T die, they win, they keep your premium, and you pay again next month.

So then, why is life insurance so important? It creates an instant estate to pay off debts, mortgages, and provide income to your dependents if you die. If you have NO ONE dependent on you for income, you may not have a need for life insurance. If you have NO ONE dependent on you for income, but you have some debt, you may want SOME life insurance to pay your debt, your funeral expenses, and your final costs if you die, so you may elect to have just a small amount of life insurance for accountability. If you desire to leave a financial legacy, such as leaving a sum of money to certain relatives, friends, or charities if you die, then you may indeed elect to cover that desire with an amount of life insurance.

If you DO have people dependent on your earned income for survival, then by all means investigate life insurance. Start with SGLI, offered through the government, and compare it with term life insurance policies offered through various military organizations. There is NO MAGIC FORMULA to dictate how much coverage you need. For a rule of thumb, tally up all of your debt, including mortgages, auto, student loan (some student loans are forgiven if you die, so you won't need to include those in this calculation!), and credit cards. Add approximately $7,500 for general funeral and administrative costs. Then decide what else you want to pre-pay if you die, including education for children, leaving lump sums to that your spouse can have no mortgage but still have income after your death for a few transitional years, and perhaps add an extra $20,000 for miscellaneous costs. That, in a nutshell, is a fairly solid swag at how much insurance coverage you need. There are PLENTY of online calculators available to predict your insurance needs. Use a couple to get a good feel for the amounts you desire.

Essentially the same argument goes for disability insurance. You are covered while active duty military, so don't sweat it now. But eventually when you leave the military, whether retirement or other, you need to consider disability insurance for the same reasons.

What if you are disabled and cannot work? Your earned income would be zero. How would you pay the mortgage? How about student loan repayments? Where would money to pay credit cards come from? How about retirement contributions, how would you pay for those?

Since SO MUCH of your financial dream depends on income during your early years, identify the need for disability insurance to cover your fixed monthly expenses as well as put food on your table each month. Then cover that amount of your household income for disability insurance. If your spouse works, look into disability income protection for your spouse's income. **This is VITAL** if you cannot pay your monthly fixed expenses on just your income, and use your spouse's income to help pay the mortgage, debts, retirement contributions, add to savings, or increase your standard of living.

Jarrod and Laurie represent a typical dual income young couple living a happy life with daughter Leslie. When son JJ is born, Jarrod and Laurie recognize that a significant life event has occurred and they need to review their family financial goals. With another mouth to feed, additional medical bills, and rising costs for diapers, current income is their first concern of a changing lifestyle.

Since Laurie is out of the workforce for a few months, Jarrod's earnings represent the sole source of income for the family. Fortunately, he has already recognized the need to reevaluate his life insurance. They decide to adjust Jarrod's life insurance death benefit upwards by $35,000 to reflect the additional costs Laurie would face should Jarrod die unexpectedly. They also wish to partially fund JJ's college education in the event Jarrod dies, so they elect to add an additional $15,000 of life insurance coverage.

Smartly, Laurie recognizes that they are now covered if Jarrod dies. But what if he lives after being incapacitated? Life insurance won't pay out, yet they will not have any family earned income. Laurie recommends they share the risk by increasing Jarrod's disability income insurance to reflect the importance of STILL having family income in the event Jarrod's disability. That's a wise move, Laurie.

Even smarter is Jarrod's decision to increase Laurie's life insurance. What if she dies? While the emotional and developmental family dynamics would be devastated, financially they would also have a problem. Jarrod's income does NOT reflect increased childcare, home upkeep, and other family matters that Laurie previously covered, so Jarrod would need to hire others to fill her shoes. That is not cheap. They decided to increase her life insurance by $50,000 after JJ's arrival to reflect additional costs Jarrod would face to continue raising the family as desired.

Wisely, Jarrod and Laurie asked their relatives, Grandma Essie and Grandpa Bruno, if there were any additional steps to take after JJ's arrival. Grandpa Bruno STRONGLY emphasized their need to update their wills to reflect JJ's birth, and to update the beneficiary status of their retirement plans, Transfer-On-Death investment accounts, Payable-On-Death savings accounts, and their life insurance policies. Grandma Essie's advice ABSOLUTELY CHANGED THEIR LIVES. Here is what she said.

When you have minor children, consider updating your life insurance beneficiary status as follows. For primary beneficiary, select 100% for your spouse. For contingent, or secondary, beneficiary, select your children for 94% of the proceeds. If you have one child, select 94%. Now that you have two children, select 47% for each. With the remaining 6%, select your guardians, Michelle and Murray, named in your will. If you trust them enough to raise your children in the event you both die, then select them for 6% total of your life insurance proceeds. Here's why.

If either of you die, your surviving spouse gets 100% of your life insurance proceeds. If you both die together, then what happens? Your children will eventually get the brunt, 94%, of your life insurance proceeds, after various court proceedings to identify, name, and appoint Michelle and Murray as the children's financial guardians. Meanwhile you IMMEDIATELY put 6% of ALL of your life insurance proceeds into Michelle's hands for the benefit of your children. After your deaths, there may well be unexpected travel involved. The children will need to be housed, clothed, fed, cared for, and they may need to travel also. Court proceedings take time and cost money.

Had you continued to name the children as 100% contingent beneficiaries, would you have been fair to Michelle and Murray? You have tied up ALL of your insurance proceeds in the courts, since minors CANNOT collect insurance proceeds. You have ignored your responsibility to take care of your children no matter what happens to you. Take some time, think it over, and consider what I have said, and if it meets your family goals then go ahead and follow my advice.

They did. And they sleep better at night.

You need to decide if Grandma Essie's advice fits your family goals and continuation plans. If it fits, implement it. If it doesn't, then at least you considered her advice, weighed its impact on your desires, and made an informed decision not to implement her sound advice. Either way you are better off as a family having discussed and analyzed this approach to continuation planning.

As a reminder, ALWAYS keep your guardian information updated in your will AND on your life insurance beneficiary forms.

While life and disability insurance reviews are important, auto and homeowner policies are more common to review. As always, you can retain, shift, or share the risks involved with auto and homeowners insurance. Minimal coverage for auto insurance will be required by state laws governing your home, but rates vary and coverage varies, so be sure to shop around by calling different companies for quotes. With auto insurance, a rule of thumb is to insure your coverage up to your net worth. Same with homeowner's insurance. If you are young and your net worth is at or near zero, you don't need a million dollars worth of coverage. If you are fifty and a millionaire, you may want extra coverage so that, in the case of an auto accident or a homeowner accident, you have shifted an appropriate amount of risk to avoid financial ruin.

A bridge between your auto and homeowners policies is a type of insurance called **Umbrella Liability insurance**. Ask about it once your net worth hits $500,000, as it can save you considerable premiums on your auto and homeowners policies while extending your coverage.

If you currently rent, it's worth considering renter's insurance to protect your belongings in the event of major catastrophes such as fire and flooding. Let's say your neighbor Greg left his stove on, and your apartment burned down, could you pay to replace all of your uniforms, stereo, watches, pendants, and belongings out of your savings account right now? If not, consider renter's insurance. For a small fee monthly it can save you thousands of dollars in replacement costs. This is a cheap means to shift the risk to an insurance company in the event of catastrophe and represents a position to consider based on feedback from your predecessors.

Actions Item #6 includes writing or updating your will and your powers of attorney. If you never had a will, pick up the phone, call your local JAG office, and make an appointment. It is free. Most likely you need a simple will. If you had a will, update it. Review your assets, decide who should get what if you die, and then make sure your wishes are reflected in your will. Your JAG office will include power of attorney forms when preparing your will. If your JAG office is too busy, consider visiting one of the online references on page 40. These are important matters, and you need to attend to them to remain accountable to your loved ones, especially after moving to a new state.

Action Item #7 is to review your life insurance needs and your disability insurance needs, if applicable. Assess how much insurance is needed as discussed in this chapter. Tailor your insurance coverage to your own needs and then adjust your coverage as necessary. There's no sense paying for too much coverage. If you need life insurance beyond SGLI, visit the companies on page 44 online for life insurance policy quotes.

Action Item #8 ties together your life insurance beneficiary selections, your will, and your Roth IRA or other retirement plans. **Review** your existing life insurance and retirement plan beneficiary status, ensuring it reflects your desires if you passed away unexpectedly last week. If it doesn't reflect your wishes, change it. Pay special attention to your guardian selection if you have small children, and apply Grandma Essie's advice from page 48 to your life insurance beneficiary choices.

Action Item #9 is to review your auto, homeowner, renter, and/or umbrella insurance coverage. Make sure you're paying as low a premium as you can for your desired coverage limits. Call your current provider and ask questions to make certain you are paying for only the coverage you need. Call other providers to get price quotes as well. If you can find the exact same coverage at a lower price, it may be worth switching.

Chapter 7

Your Personal Financial Plan

We all need goals if we are going to strive to achieve anything. Otherwise we wind up aimlessly floating through life. You wouldn't be in our all-volunteer military today if you didn't have some type of goals and saw the military as a means to achieve these goals, whether for a full career or as a stepping stone to a future non-military career. Financial goals are no different, and by identifying short and long-term goals, and then by prioritizing these goals, you will be leaps and bounds ahead of track to achieve them.

So grab your most recent Leave and Earnings Statement (LES), a pen, paper, a calculator, and your corresponding monthly checking account statement, and let's get started.

First you need to identify your financial goals. Typical short-term goals include living on less than you earn each pay period, setting up an emergency savings account for the emergencies life throws at us, and buying a car. Long-term goals typically include saving for a house downpayment, investing for retirement, and funding a child's college education.

Now you can write down your financial goals. All of them, short and long term. Go back and prioritize them. Would you rather own the latest cell phone or own a home in 3 years? Would you rather have a comfortable retirement or drive a new car throughout your life? You need to ask yourself these questions as you prioritize your goals. You need to recognize the tradeoffs associated with a fixed salary income. There is only so much money coming in each month, and funding every goal right now may not feasible, so prioritize. **Financial planning** is the process of identifying and prioritizing financial goals, gathering information on where you are now and where you want to be, analyzing various methods to achieve these goals, implementing chosen ideas, then consistently monitoring and updating these methods and making adjustments as economic conditions and tax laws change. You have a wonderful resource called the **2005 Financial Planning Guide** printed each year by the Financial Services Publishing Company in Alexandria, VA. It explains basics of saving, investing, insurance, and SBP for all military personnel, and provides tremendous information and resources as well. It's available FREE OF CHARGE online as well, and can be downloaded from the www.afba.com website.

Financial planning is no different, in theory, than driving a car. See the connection? Does this help empower you that YOU CAN ACHIEVE YOUR GOALS? Great! Let's keep going.

Your second step is to find out WHERE your money goes. For the previous month, identify your gross pay from your LES statement. This will be comprised of your base pay for your rank, any allowances, special pays, incentive pays, and bonuses. Then note the federal income, FICA, Medicare, and Social Security taxes that are withheld. Did you realize that you are paying these from each paycheck? This is the IRS-style investment method discussed in the previous chapters. See, it DOES work! Also note any allotments you pay directly from your income. This may include uniform reimbursement, charitable donations, Thrift Savings Plan contributions, and federal loan repayments.

Next, after your allotments are deducted from your gross pay, you have identified your NET income. Divided by 2, since you get paid twice each month, this represents the amount you have direct deposited to your checking account each payday. This is YOUR money! This is where YOU get to decide HOW MUCH you want to keep! This is where YOU can choose to pay YOURSELF if you so desire.

Without looking at your checkbook, write down how much you pay for housing (if living off base), car payment, furniture payment, credit cards, layaway payments, and any debts that you owe. All set? Let's again, from memory, record approximately how much you spend on groceries, uniforms, dining out, sodas, coffee, tobacco, entertainment, and club dues. How much is left? Write down how much you would LIKE to save each month, how much you may need for emergencies, and how much you want to PAY YOURSELF out of EACH PAYCHECK because, as you know, a PART of ALL YOU EARN is YOURS to KEEP.

Here's the eye-opening part: go through your checking account statement, and identify, honestly, WHERE your money went last month. For BONUS points, feel welcome to add a column on the far right end of your checking statement titled "N or W." This translates to "Need or Want," meaning did you NEED that item or did you WANT that item? Mark them appropriately, line by line, with honesty.

Now let's compare your **intended spending** you're your **actual spending** to identify your spending habits. How closely does your ACTUAL spending match your INTENDED spending? What "emergencies" came up during the month that required additional money, including flat tires, auto repairs, home repairs, or annual dues coming due? How much did you REALLY spend on entertainment?

How much did you spend on groceries? How much did you direct towards savings?

No one will EVER watch you money as closely as YOU will. So how are you doing? Are you on track? Are you on budget? Is your money being spent AS YOU DESIRE? Are you depleting savings? Are you paying YOURSELF? Or did you spend MORE that you made, financing the difference on a credit card by identifying an increasing balance?

GOOD OR BAD, **LET THIS BE YOUR WAKEUP CALL.** If you are already on track, then you are reinforcing your cashflow. If you are NOT on track, then let this be a turning point. Let's turn this around.

STOP the habits that are NOT moving you towards your goals, and **START** the proven habits that WILL take you where you want to go.

If you want to spend LESS than you earn, and save (or invest) the difference, let's implement the IRS method for savings. **Start an allotment of $25 per payday into a savings account immediately.** This will ensure you pay yourself SOMETHING right off the bat. If you do not have consumer debt, then congratulations, and consider GIVING YOURSELF A $25 PER PAYDAY PAYRAISE.

Review your "Need or Want" column, and decide what purchases you can DO WITHOUT in the future. Next time you "spontaneously" spend $50 on music at the exchange, consider only buying 1 CD instead of 3. Change your behavior. Recognize what isn't working, stop doing that, and start doing what your predecessors recommend!

Remind yourself to recognize your past spending habits, identify "Need" versus "Want" spending, and make appropriate decisions TODAY to keep on track for your goals. One of the strongest feedback items involved taping a sticky note to your mirror in your bathroom so you can see it each morning. Two suggestions from your predecessors served them well. The first veteran, former Air Force pilot Mike, simply wrote "Today I will RECOGNIZE that I am buying a WANT item, and then think twice to make sure I really want it before buying it." The second veteran, former Army nurse Kona, wrote a simple list of two goals onto a sticky note, as follows:

1. Save $100 per paycheck for House Downpayment
2. Invest $50 per paycheck for my Roth IRA in my American Century Mid-Cap Growth Fund

These were the only two items on her "list." In actuality, she had already automated these tasks, but she wrote back that this simple reminder on her mirror REINFORCED that she was moving TOWARDS her goals each payday. It also reinforced unintended spending, making her think twice prior to making spontaneous consumer purchases. Needless to say, she is continuing to add to these amounts monthly after employing the Rule of 1/3, and as of January 2005 she deposits $225 per month into her house downpayment account while MAXIMIZING her Roth IRA contribution (currently $333.33 per month!). **This works**.

Your final step is to periodically update and monitor your progress towards your goals. Build upon your past successes, using the same techniques to assist you now. At some point you had money in your pocket prior to entering the military. Did you rake leaves to earn money? Babysit? Mow lawns? Work in fast food? Did you receive an allowance? At some point you either had money in your pocket or in a bank account. How did you stop from spending it the moment it was in your hand? How did you keep that money in your pocket overnight? There is no doubt you wanted and desired many, many different things, yet you did not spend that money that night on them. You kept it in your pocket. Let's improve on this step.

Continue to pay yourself. Keep adding to that allotment from your military paycheck. Keep a part of all you earn. You deserve it. This is the fundamental base to achieve your future financial goals, be they short-term or long-term. Start the habit of paying yourself first, then spend what is left over on your consumer items. This keeps you in control of your finances. This keeps you on track for your financial goals. This enables you to keep the saving habits in place to achieve any financial goal you desire.

Action Item #10 is to write down your personal financial plan. Hand-write it on paper at first, following the outline in your 2005 Financial Planning guide mentioned on page 54. Identify and prioritize your financial goals, gather information on where you are now and where you want to be, analyze methods to achieve these goals, implement chosen ideas, then consistently monitor and update these methods. By taking time to write down your goals, you are solidifying your desire to achieve them. This original plan becomes your road map on your path to all of your financial goals.

Section 2

MISSION
Your Re-Enlistment Decisions
(Should I Stay or Should I Go?)

Continue these 5 habits:
1. IRS-style savings account
2. IRS-style investment account
3. Continue funding your Roth IRA
4. Continue Rule of 1/3 for pay raises
5. Consider buying a home

Update these 5 documents:
1. Simple will
2. Power of Attorney for Finances
3. Power of Attorney for Healthcare
4. Emergency data sheet
5. Update beneficiaries on SGLI life insurance, TSP, and Roth IRA accounts

Read these 3 books from your local library:
1. Landlording by Leigh Robinson
2. The Courage To Be Rich by Suze Orman
3. The Midas Touch by John Train

Chapter 8

Total Military Compensation

Let's say you're earning $3,000 monthly as a 23-year old E-5 in the Coast Guard stationed in Virginia Beach, VA. You have 5 years of service and you are considering reenlisting for another 6 years. You have a job offer from a defense contractor for $42,000 annually. You will perform essentially the same job as you're performing now, on the same equipment, and you'll be paid an additional 20% for deploying. Should you take it?

What is the line of thinking that should ALWAYS come with these decisions? Our veterans replied OVERWHELMINGLY to consider ALL of these factors before making the leap, as the grass is ALWAYS greener on the "civilian side" when you are making your decision.

Take some time and imagine yourself at age 85, sitting at a kitchen table. As you look back at your life, what are you glad you did? What do you wish you had done? Would you be happy following a path to finish your military career? Would you get tired of collecting those retirement checks every month starting at age 38? Are you enjoying your life now?

If you enjoy the camaraderie of the military, recognize the unique excitement in your job, exude pride to wear the uniform, seek new challenges ahead, and generally see yourself happiest by fulfilling your military career, then consider staying in the military and be thankful for your current opportunities.

1. You have tremendous equipment, computer systems, and unlimited technical training regardless of your line of work.
2. You have access to free medical care, and that's nothing to sneeze about when compared to civilian group health policies.
3. You have relatively free dental care.
4. You have dirt-cheap SGLI life insurance with no war clause.
5. You have solid disability insurance at no cost.
6. You have tax-free allowances paid to you
7. Your federal pay avoids Virginia state income tax while on active duty
8. You have access to all kinds of beneficial counseling at no charge through your family service centers
9. You enjoy the unique camaraderie found in military units that forms life-long friendships and provides common grounds for future friendships

If you have goals that you will not achieve by continuing in the military, then make sure financially you consider the following items.

1. For the salary offered, subtract your higher federal income taxes payable (100% of this salary and bonuses are taxable)
2. Subtract your state of Virginia income taxes payable
3. Subtract your annual health insurance premiums
4. Subtract your annual dental insurance premiums
5. Subtract your annual short-term disability insurance premiums

6. Subtract your annual long-term disability insurance premiums
7. Add in the retirement plan match, if any, as there was no match for your military TSP.

Are you still seeing a higher income now? When you compare apples to apples, if you are making additional money, have you considered the following?

1. Subtract the cost of a new civilian wardrobe
2. Subtract the additional cost of commuting to work
3. Subtract the cost of parking, if applicable
4. Subtract the cost of grocery shopping in grocery stores rather than the commissary

Now how are things stacking up? Is it worth it? **Only you can tell.** Will you have additional housing costs? Will this company offer to move you? You and you alone have the final say in any proposed job acceptance, and we hope you benefit from reviewing what your predecessors went through prior to making your final decision.

Most of your predecessors responded that they wish they had stayed in the military. Here are the top four reasons combed from their various responses:

1. They missed the camaraderie of working with great people towards a worthy goal
2. They missed the challenges presented by the unique circumstances under which our military operates, including deployments, travel, and training
3. They viewed 10 years as "forever" when they were young, but now view it as a drop in the bucket
4. They realize now that had they stayed in, **retired at 38 with a pension**, then gone to work at what they wanted, they could have had years of fun in their chosen line of work rather than learning to love the job they had

Only you know whether it's worth it or not. Take heed what your seniors say, for they are living history books. They have already walked in your moccasins. They have faced your decisions and, good or bad, are sharing their thoughts with you.

It's worth addressing one of the most appealing reasons for getting out of the military after your first tour. It's the chance to earn more money while staying in one place (no deployments). While this topic is addressed in the previous paragraphs, what about the appeal of self-employment?

Many predecessors that took the self-employment route reminded us that you will put in more hours than you think, you won't initially earn as much as you think, and you will be disappointed in how many extra expenses you incur, including additional self-employment taxes, health insurance, professional insurance, state fees, county fees, and city fees. What helpful tips did they offer, especially to those of you pursuing service or advice-based businesses?

Advice-based self-employed businesses, including post-military self-employed financial advisors and insurance agents (more than half of your responses were from individuals in this field), are approximately 22% more profitable than standard sole proprietorships. They recommend using a Limited Liability Corporation (LLC) titling for legal protection if it is offered in your state, so at least consider it for your business. They recommend pricing your time according to a unique formula to account for lost "administrative, bookkeeping, and training" time. And they recommend you retain a bookkeeper experienced in quarterly tax estimates, state income tax laws (if applicable), and recordkeeping.

The unique pricing recommendation calls for additional explanation. Successful feedback came in the form of billing based on 4 quarterly 10-week periods of 40 hours per week. When questioned, they responded it is necessary to account for lost **training, marketing, and administrative** time. This accounting allowed them to set QUARTERLY goals, focus on the next quarter, and stay motivated.

Based on this successful theory, they divided **each quarter** into 10 weeks of 40 hours each. They divided their annual desired salary by 1,600 to account for the total billing hours recognized, 400 hours per quarter for 4 quarters. They multiplied this number by 1.5 to account for a 50% cost of overhead. They multiplied this number by 1.5 to account for self-employment taxes and rising health insurance costs. This became their **required hourly rate** to achieve their goals.

As an example, Mario decides to leave the Navy and start a deep salvage diving consulting business in Fort Lauderdale based on his expertise as a diver in the Navy. If he wants to earn **$60,000** this year, he should divide that figure by 1,600 hours per year, arriving at $37.50 per hour. Then he needs to multiply by 1.5 to account for business overhead (advertising, rent, utilities) to arrive at $56.25 per hour. After that, he still needs to multiply this number by 1.5 again to account for self-employment taxes and health insurance costs, which amounts to $84.38. His final hourly charge, based on 1,600 billing hours per year, is **$84.38** per hour. That sounds expensive, but after accounting for overhead, taxes, health insurance, and other costs, it has proven a successful means to accurately predict HOW MUCH to **VALUE YOUR SERVICES** if you want to achieve a certain salary.

In short, if Mario wants to earn $60,000, he needs to bill $84.38 each hour for 40 hours per week, 10 weeks per quarter, 4 quarters per year, to achieve his goal, based on paying average overhead and tax expenses. Sounds daunting? Better to find out NOW rather than find out

LATER. Take heed of your seniors who have been through this, and consider this PRIOR to plunking down your own money, becoming your own boss, and finding out later you wish you had charged more.

Action Item #11 is to consider ALL factors prior to making your decision to stay in the military or to get out. There are a considerable number of factors to consider, and a number of veterans who did get out wish they had stayed in to at least finish 20 years of service. Healthcare could play a vital role in your decision in the future, so pay special attention to healthcare costs for your family before getting out. In the end it is YOUR decision to stay or go. Either way, it makes sound financial sense to continue your fundamental approach to savings, investing, and spending whether you stay or whether you go. Anchors aweigh!

Chapter 9

Your Mortgage Matters

Whether you stay in the military or join the civilian workforce, proven advice regarding your mortgage remains important financially. While your employment decision matters significantly, so does your decision on how to pay on your mortgage.

What's the smartest way to pay back a mortgage? Pay it off early with no pre-payment penalties. We're not talking about paying off a 30-year mortgage in 9 months, but we are talking about paying off extra principal every month.

If you have a $100,000, 30-year mortgage at 6% interest, how much do you think you'd pay in interest alone, besides paying off the principal of $100,000? If you paid the $600 mortgage every month for 30 years, you'd have paid $115,838 in interest alone. Ouch. That's another house, and then some. So how can we save thousands on a mortgage?

If you pay an extra $50 each payment, and direct it towards principal reduction, it has a tremendous impact on your mortgage repayment.

For our example, if we paid the $600 mortgage payment, and added $50 every payment specified towards paying on the principal, we'd pay off the house in 24 years and 7 months, and we'd pay $24,736 **less** in interest.

That's quite a savings, isn't it? So if you're house-hunting, and a realtor says you can afford a $120,000 mortgage, why not stick with a $100,000 mortgage, keep your cashflow flexible, and use the extra money to **pay it off early?**

Plenty of veterans added comments about mortgages and whether to pay them off early or not. Many went into detail about the time value of money, hinting that no one should pay early on a 30-year mortgage as the payments in the last few years are made with much cheaper dollars, eroded by inflation, than originally calculated. Others argued that paying off a mortgage is more of an emotional decision than a financial decision. Our viewpoint is that it can be shown financially what the effect of paying off a mortgage means to cashflow, and what the opportunity cost of adding extra principal payments means to investors.

Gabe and Danielle buy a new home using a large downpayment and financing $100,000 at 6% with a fixed rate 30-year mortgage. They are in the 25% marginal income tax bracket and both are on active duty in Washington, where there is no state income tax. After closing on their home, their Uncle Bob dies, leaving them $10,000 in his will. At current interest rates, Gabe and Danielle decide they can buy a 5-year Certificate of Deposit at their bank that pays 5% interest, they can invest in a balanced no-load mutual fund that historically pays 5% in capital gains over time, or they can pay ahead on their mortgage. Which is the best option for them, with all other variable equal?

If they invest in the CD, they will earn $500 interest on their money in the first year. They will need to pay income taxes on this money, and being in the 25% bracket they will owe an additional $125 in taxes, reducing their net first-year gain to $375. Their net after-tax rate of return is not 5%, it is 3.75%. This is true for the remaining 4 years on the CD term also.

If Gabe and Danielle invest in the balanced no-load mutual fund, and earn 5% on their money annually, it will be taxed at long-term capital gains rates when they sell it in 5 years, so their net tax due will be only 15% on their earnings. This represents a 4.25% net after tax rate of return on their money if indeed their mutual fund performs to its historical figure and returns an even 5% during that timeframe.

If Gabe and Danielle pay ahead on their mortgage with this windfall, they avoid paying interest on that $10,000 in principal for the remainder of the mortgage. While this won't change their monthly payment, it does significantly shorten the term of their loan. Since their mortgage rate is 6% and they are in the 25% marginal tax bracket, their effective after-tax return is 4.5%. While it remains a partially emotional decision to pay down a mortgage, it actually represents a financially prudent decision, locking in an automatic 4.5% after tax rate of return on their money. This is a comparison means to consider in order to more equally level the playing field when comparing investments.

Isn't it amazing how a seemingly small additional payment can pay off a loan so quickly? This works on an automobile loan also, just remember to specify additional principal payment on your loan coupon.

The best news is that **YOU** don't need to pay anyone a fee to turn your current 30-year mortgage into a 24-year mortgage. **You** can decide on your own by sending in additional principal payments, and watch the savings begin right away.

It isn't always prudent to pay as much as possible on your mortgage early, as this is illiquid savings. Should you need money for an emergency, but you don't have a full emergency savings account funded yet, then you'll have a difficult time pulling money out of your home equity. So please don't go overboard on this example of paying off your mortgage early by putting every dollar of savings into debt reduction.

You'll have more "wiggle room" if you continue to finance other investment vehicles, such as mutual funds and retirement programs, in addition to paying off your mortgage early. Imagine retirement where you have military retirement pay coming in, social security coming in, and NO MORTGAGE PAYMENT! Not a bad way to enjoy your golden years, as many current veterans are finding out.

This concept is so important it bears repeating: **Paying rent secures another's financial future, but paying your own mortgage secures your own.**

You had some insightful stories in your emails regarding interest-only mortgages. While this will help you afford a higher priced home, it may not be in your best interest to finance your home this way. This IS an appropriate method to finance a home under two conditions historically. First, if you are 90% certain of significant pay increases during the next 3 years, then consider an interest-only mortgage. Second, if you are 90% certain you will sell this home in the next 5 years, consider an interest-only loan. As always, ensure there is no prepayment penalty if you DO choose to add principal to payments, as is recommended.

At some point it may be worth your while to pay principal payments on an interest-only loan. Most common is if you financed a home with an interest-only mortgage and decide to keep the home in retirement. As interest rates rise there will come a point where your interest rate on a variable rate loan is higher than the long-term historical rate of return for higher risk investments such as large capital stocks. When that day comes, you are guaranteed to lock in a fixed percentage return, after tax, by paying ahead on your mortgage and avoiding the interest due on principal.

As an example, let's take the case of siblings Linda and Lenny. Lenny is a 29-year old Army E-6, and his sister Linda is a 28-year old Air Force E-6. Both live in the San Diego area, each has 11 years of service and both plan on staying in until retirement. Neither is married, and they each want to buy a home, but neither can afford to on their own salary. Together they earn enough to qualify for a $500,000 mortgage, but have different views on the best type of mortgage for the San Diego home they wish to purchase.

Lenny leans towards a 40-year interest-only mortgage, citing statistics on housing price increases in the last 10 years. He thinks they are foolish to consider paying principal, and views the interest-only loan as the best means to buy this home. Lenny wants to sell the home in 9 years at retirement, take their profits, and move on. Linda thinks they should get a conventional 30-year VA loan, locking in a 6% interest rate for 30 years. She feels that, since interest rates are at 40-year lows, they should lock in because they want to keep this home, pay it off, and live in it forever. Who is right and why?

Does it surprise you that each of them is correct for their goals and timeframes for the home?

Let's look only at principal and interest for these loan amounts, as you will agree that property taxes and homeowner's insurance are equal in either scenario and therefore can be removed from this comparison. Also, let's assume the price of this home doubles in 10 years, will sell for exactly $1 million, and each sibling will therefore owe no federal income tax due to the $250,000 gain exemption for individuals living in the home.

In Lenny's mind, an interest-only loan allows them to make minimal mortgage payments, forgo paying down on principal, and pocket their gain in 10 years when they sell.

This approach is solid IF interest rates remain low. Interest-only loans typically are variable rates, commonly locked in for a period of 3 to 5 years. After that, the interest rates will adjust to market conditions. That is where the danger lies, as no one can predict interest rate movements with exact precision.

While there may be a cap or limit to the jump in interest rates, this may cause a significant increase in mortgage payments also. If Lenny accepts a 40-year, interest only variable rate loan, with a 3-year lock at 5%, the interest portion of their payment will be just $2,083 per month. After 3 years, if the interest rate resets to 7%, then their payment jumps to $2,917 per month. After 3 years, if the interest rate leaps to 9%, their interest payment would increase to $3,750 per month. These are the significant risks Lenny is willing to accept in exchange for a lower initial payment.

Linda feels differently. Since she plans to keep this home forever, she sees the benefit in paying down the mortgage until they owe nothing on the home. Her traditional approach means paying higher mortgage payments, as a portion will pay down the interest also. Knowing she wants to pay the home off someday, Linda may even ask her brother to pay extra principal on the mortgage every month, thus turning a 30-year mortgage into a 15-year mortgage through extra principal payments. She is excited to lock in these historically low rates, as she knows her pay will only go up, so the first year will be the toughest for them financially. With a 30-year 6% mortgage, their monthly principal and interest portion of their payment is $2,983 and it remains constant regardless of interest rate movements in the future.

By paying $2,983 monthly, after 30 years of payments they will owe nothing on the mortgage and own their home free and clear. By adding $50 each to extra principal payments each month, they will cut the term of their loan down below 26 years. Linda leans towards the more conservative approach of locking in a low interest rate for the life of the loan and paying ahead on the principal.

Eventually Lenny and Linda agree on a mortgage and purchase the home. They are wiser for understanding their mortgage options, analyzing which one best fits their goals for ownership timeframe, salary increases, and future relocation projections out of the area. There are all types of variations on mortgages, so don't hesitate to ask for other alternatives that may better fit your situation.

One other common alternative is becoming more popular as interest rates rise from these historical lows. You may want to consider an assumable mortgage for your home. This allows you tremendous flexibility should you sell your home in just a few years. Here's how it works.

Sue and Al buy a $250,000 home in Mayport, Florida, with a VA mortgage. They lock in a 30-year rate of 6% on an assumable loan, meaning their monthly principal and interest portion of the payment is $1,491. Four years later, Sue gets orders to California and they sell their home. New mortgages are offered at 8% for 30 years because interest rates have risen since Sue and Al bought their home. This translates to a principal and interest payment of $1,822 per month, which deters a lot of buyers. Keep in mind that the mortgage is backed by the value of the real estate, so a mortgage is transportable if the new buyers qualify. Since Sue and Al were wise enough to purchase an assumable mortgage, they can have potential buyers assume their mortgage when they buy the home and pay Sue and Al the difference in price. Sue and Al will attract a LOT more buyers with an assumable loan if interest rates rise. This is a technique you may wish to consider if purchasing a home in the next 6 months.

Why does this work in your favor? As the cost of money gets cheaper, meaning as interest rates fall, there is a natural tendency for housing prices to historically rise. A buyer that can afford to spend $1,500 per month on principal and interest payments can buy a $280,000 home at 5% interest for 30 years. The same buyer, still paying the same $1,500 per month on principal and interest, can only afford a $206,000 mortgage if interest rates rise to 8%. For the same mortgage payment, it buys less as interest rates rise. That's because more of the payment is going towards interest, and less towards principal. Sue and Al are just tilting the odds in their favor by locking in a low interest rate now on an assumable loan in order to increase the buyers who can afford it if they sell when interest rates rise. This is good, solid, fundamental economic thinking on their part, and you will be wise to consider this type of assumable mortgage while interest rates are low.

Action Item #12 is to sit down and analyze your current mortgage. Is it working for you? How can you best achieve your goals with your current mortgage? Should you be paying ahead on the principal? Should you pay off your mortgage with other assets if you have them? Should you be considering refinancing to lock in a lower rate? If you plan on selling in a few years, is it financially worth refinancing now? These are the questions to ask yourself, and your mortgage broker, as you re-read this chapter. Paying smartly on your mortgage is vital to long-term financial health.

Chapter 10

How Do YOU Stack Up?

We all, from time to time, want to know where we stand relative to our peers. To view how you've done financially, flip ahead to Appendix D and see how you stack up against your peers by age group and by net worth. Pay special attention to the verbiage at the end of Appendix D also. You are receiving below-average incomes to reflect your impending pension upon retirement. You aren't TRULY vested until year 20, when you become eligible to retire, early retirement offers not withstanding.

Have you ever heard the old saying, 'If you don't know jewelry, then know your jeweler', credited to the ageless Mae West? The same principle holds true for finances. **Stop asking others who are struggling** to live paycheck to paycheck how to save and invest money. Instead, **start asking those who are financially sound**, and sincerely ask them how they learned the skills to live on less than they earn.

Every military unit has senior enlisted and senior officer personnel that have success stories and horror stories about finances. Why not begin by asking within your own unit? All stories, good or bad, can **have a lasting impact**.

For example, why use the services of an auto mechanic for a simple oil change? It's not that difficult to change your oil in your car. You can choose to do it. It requires changing into suitable clothing, turning a few nuts, changing a filter, pouring oil, and disposing of the used oil in a safe way, ensuring all plugs are replaced, and then changing out of your clothes.

It is a learned skill indeed, to learn how to change your own oil. And yet millions of people every week will pay to have their oil changed. Why? It saves time, effort, and provides peace of mind. Even if you have the time and knowledge to change it yourself, you may lack the desire. If you have the knowledge and desire, you may lack the time. These principles can be paralleled to money management. That's exactly what reading, exploring, and asking questions can do for you; teach you how to manage your own money. The exact same principles apply.

If you think that all you need is a high-paying job with fringe benefits and you'll be financially set for life, **you need to rethink your strategy**. Here are a few well-documented examples to tuck away.

Have you ever read about a professional baseball player from the mid-1980's? Here's a man earning over $1 million per year, and yet he ends up near bankruptcy. Let's look at his financial behavior and see if it violates our "strong financial suggestions" for wise money management.

He purchased multiple high-cost, high-end automobiles, which of course leads to high maintenance, high insurance costs, high security costs, and high storage costs. It was documented that he'd send a batboy for a sandwich, give him a $100 bill, and let the boy keep the change as a tip. He purchased an expensive home, again costing him high property taxes, high upkeep, and of course a lower-than-expected resale value due to its custom-built specifications. In summary, he lived high on the hog, at a rate not sustainable because he spent more than he earned on depreciating assets.

Do you recall the rise of a musical sensation in the late 1980's? Here's a tremendous musical talent that rose to national prominence in the late 1980's and early 90's, selling millions of albums and selling out each tour stop. He built a $10 million home (think of the upkeep!), paid salaries to dozens of performers for his tour, bought racehorses (more upkeep), and was a well-documented spender. It wasn't long before the music sales fell off, the money stopped rolling in, and this individual declared bankruptcy.

These stories are important because they show that even high-income level entertainers need **to respect the laws of money management**. They are not infallible to the laws of prudent spending; namely, spending less than you earn, and ensuring a part of all you earn is yours to keep.

Clearly, **income level does not guarantee financial stability.** Had either entertainer spent less than they'd earned, and set money aside as capital from which to live off the earnings, they'd be financially better off today. Once again, by insisting that a part of all they earn is theirs to keep, they would never be near bankruptcy without violating that "strong financial suggestion."

Let's talk about "play money", also known as disposable income. If you put part of each paycheck towards your retirement, part towards your emergency money, part towards your current living style, and still have some left over, that's for the fun stuff. Won't it be more enjoyable to spend extra money on a vacation, big-screen TV, sporting event, opera, or clothing once you've taken care of your long and short-term goals with your serious money?

How do you get started? **Start right now**, this very minute. Tell yourself you **CHOOSE** not to spend your money on this item or that item right now. Yes, you **COULD** purchase that $12 stuffed animal for your child because the child wants it, but you **CHOOSE** not to at this time.

Does this sound like a classic **WANT** versus **NEED** discussion? Does your child NEED another stuffed toy? Or would the money saved by NOT spending on a want item be better saved for later use? Only you can decide for your own situation.

Set a goal. Any goal. What do you want? What do you crave? You can achieve it. You can have it. It will take some work, some sacrifice, and some discipline to achieve. But in the end, **you know it's achievable**.

That's what makes America so wonderful.

See. Do. Enjoy. Absorb. Play. And know that while you're doing this, your serious money is hard at work for you, ensuring you can see, do, play, etc. well into the future.

Action Item #13 is to flip ahead to Appendix D and see how you stack up. You can monitor your progress going forward by noting your financial net worth according to salary and according to age. Don't forget the tremendous impact your retirement pay has on effective net worth. If your retirement pay stream of income were discounted and sold as a lump sum, you would count that lump sum as a part of your net worth. You would be exchanging income for an asset at that point, and it is by no means recommended. But for comparison purposes only, can you see how your military retirement income stream truly boosts your net worth at a relatively young retirement age? Awesome! Thanks to former Marine wife Purie for this insight via her daughter.

Chapter 11

Proven Techniques to KEEP You On Track For Your Goals

Stop and ponder this question: what is your greatest financial asset? Is it your home? Your retirement plan? Your pension? Believe it or not it's your **earnings capability**, also know as your ability to earn money.

If you earn $30,000 per year, then over the next 20 years, excluding pay increases and bonuses, you'll earn **$600,000!**

Now, how much of that do you intend to keep? How much will you set aside for your short and long-term financial goals? How much will you spend on appreciating assets, and how much on depreciating assets? The choice, as always, is up to **YOU**.

How can you **improve** your earnings capability? You can seek formal schooling, and attend seminars, workshops, and courses related to your current job. You can learn **on the job**, seeking tips from those you work with and admire. You can read books, magazines, watch videos, and download all kinds of material to study on your own. Anything you learn to apply will contribute towards making you better in your field.

If you earn a set salary, then in order to save more money you can only decrease your spending.

If you can **increase your salary**, however, then you can keep your spending the same, save the difference in your higher earnings, and invest it towards your long-term goals. Now, if you have the discipline, you can combine these two attributes to **turbo-power your investments.**

Just suppose you earned a salary increase of $1 per hour at work. If you work an average 40-hour workweek, then you'll earn an extra $160 monthly. What if you increased your standard of living by $53, paid $53 in additional income taxes, and increased your long-term savings by $53? You'd have **a higher current income**, yet you'd be on a faster track to achieve your longer-term goals too. That's the **best of both worlds!!**

So next time you earn a pay raise, it will be wise to set **one third** of the weekly increase aside for income taxes, invest **one third** for your short or long-term goals (or pay down debt with one third, including your mortgage), and you can still increase your standard of living by one third. Everyone wins!

What good is foregoing current spending your entire life, saving and investing every nickel, and then when you pass away your estate is cut in half by estate taxes? Or even worse, what if your children are spenders, and blow through every penny of their inheritance within 5 years of your death? Would it have been worth it?

Take some time and educate your heirs on successful money management. Studies show that 88% of wealth disappears through aggressive spending after just 2 generations. If that doesn't motivate you to educate your heirs on money management, nothing will.

Philosophy of life has a lot to do with financial success too. **Spend now versus save for later.** Remember Aesop's Fables? The ant works all summer to gather and store food for the winter, while the grasshopper plays all summer, and subsequently finds himself without food for the winter.

Well, who are the ants among us?   Who are the grasshoppers?

Are you a grasshopper because you want to be, or did you just wake up one day and discover you had played a lot and the autumn air had already arrived?

Here's the best part of all: **YOU have full control** to decide whether to behave like the ant or the grasshopper. It's **YOUR** choice. **YOU** make the call.

The good news is that **you can change your habits** when you really want to, and start gathering food no matter how late into autumn you think it is.   After all, you'll still be further ahead by gathering SOME food than you would by continuing to play.

Army veteran Stan wants to buy a Christmas tree from a neighborhood sales lot this year.   Last year's trees were priced from $15 to $40, so this year he intends to buy a $15 tree again.   He goes down to the lot with $15 in his hand, only to find the prices have increased to $18 for the cheapest tree this year.   **Welcome to the world of inflation, Stan.**

If you think Christmas tree prices have increased, wait until you talk with someone who takes medicine daily, and talk to them about the price of refills. This is the first part of a paired concept, so let's review the second, and then we'll tie them together.

Once you receive your paycheck, what do you do with it?   Do you deposit it in a bank or credit union, and then start paying bills and spending from there?   Is your "disposable income" defined as what's left over after you're done paying bills?

Well, let's turn this situation around.   You worked all week, and **you deserve to have a portion of this money set aside for YOUR future spending**.   So let's take ten percent on payday and transfer it to our savings account. Then let's start paying bills and setting aside amounts for the upcoming rent payment, or auto insurance payment, etc. Once we've done this for 3 consecutive paychecks, congratulations, we've lived on less than we earned!

Now, if you have to use some of this savings for an emergency, don't sweat it, these things happen. But see if you aren't able to save an addition couple of dollars each month now that you've successfully become a saver.

This money you've transferred to a savings account, does the bank keep it in a vault, neatly stacked with your name on it? No, they are using **your** money to earn money for the **bank**. Where do you go to get a car loan? The bank. What interest rate do they charge? Let's say 8%. How about credit cards, how much interest do they charge on those? 14%? 18%? 24%? Banks also are investors in the economy of stocks, bonds, bills, and notes. These investments historically yield from 5-11%. And what about mortgages, what are those rates typically? Between 7% and 9%?

So, if the bank is paying you 2% on your checking and savings accounts, and then loans out the money to others at 8%, 18%, and 24%, invests in stocks, bonds and mutual funds earning 8%, plus is collecting Automated Teller Machine (ATM) fees, non-sufficient fund fees, overdrawn account fees, etc, then is it any wonder why banks have beautiful marble lobbies and spacious business buildings?

What can you do about it? You can stop letting banks earn the high rates, and you can earn them yourself to stay ahead of inflation.

Here's where we tie our last two topics together. How can you **stay ahead of inflation?** By earning rates of return on your money that are **higher** than the rate of inflation!

You can cut out the bank in this loop, and accept the benefits of higher earnings on your money for accepting the responsibility of managing it.

You can earn inflation-beating rates of return by investing in mutual funds and bonds through your retirement plan at work, whether it's a 401(k), Tax Sheltered Annuity, Thrift Savings Plan, or other form of retirement savings vehicle. This is the place to be for your long-term savings goals.

If inflation averaged 3.5% annually, which it roughly has the past 40 years, and your passbook savings rate averaged 3.5%, then any money you put away would be treading water. If you earned 3% in a savings account, you would have less purchasing power each year and you'd be sinking. A 5% return on your investments and savings would provide you with positive results, staying ahead of inflation, but not by much.

If you can stay ahead of inflation every year with your savings and investments, then you're bound to achieve increased earning power over time.

How do we make our current financial decisions? Are they in line with our goals? Are we buying need items, or want items? And yes, it does make a difference.

Would you do it all over again? Ask an **eighty year old** what they'd do over again. Marry the same person? Stay at home with the kids? Work and let the kids fend for themselves? Earn an extra ten thousand bucks?

We all have a certain timeframe we're blessed with. How about making the most of it, and letting some of your money work for you while you're enjoying what you do? If you have steadily saved money, invested it, and are reaping the benefits of your investments, then how can you **pass this knowledge on** to others? By being patient and truthful when someone asks you questions about wealth.

Action Item #14 revolves around investments. Are you fully involved in your investing? Is it wise to become more aware of the fees you are paying to invest? If you pick your own stocks, are you using a deep discount broker to make your trades? If you pick your own mutual funds, are you paying sales fees for load funds, or are you rewarding yourself and investing in no-load mutual funds? It's time to update your asset allocation and realign your allocation for your financial goal timeframes.

As always, look at your investment decisions as business decisions. If you bought a stock for a reason, is it time to sell for another reason? Are you on track to achieve your goal in the first place? Was it a short term goal? Was it a long term goal? Have you accounted for inflation and taxes? Are you minimizing your investment costs? By now you are getting a handle on investments, savings, and achieving financial goals. You are gaining experience, both good and bad, that you can carry forward to become a more efficient investor in the future. Keep up the good work.

Section 3

APPROACH
Pre-Retirement Planning for Years 15-20+ of Military Service

Discuss and update these 4 areas:
1. Wills, POAs, Emergency data sheet
2. Update beneficiaries on SGLI life insurance, Thrift Savings Plan, and Roth IRA accounts
3. Pre-retirement physical
4. Survivor Benefit Plan consideration

Continue these 5 habits NOW:
1. IRS-style investment account
2. Roth IRA
3. Continue Rule of 1/3 for Pay Raises
4. Contribute to Retirement Plans at New Job
5. Apply for Disability Insurance at New Job

Read these 3 publications from your local library
1. <u>Just Give Me The Answers</u> by Sheryl Garrett
2. <u>Military Survival Guide to Financial Planning</u> by Douglas Rothman
3. <u>One Up on Wall Street</u> by Peter Lynch

Chapter 12

Military Pension Election Decisions

Protecting your pension is one of the **MOST OVERLOOKED** decisions pre-retirement families face. Back by popular demand, here is an analysis that other veterans appreciated immensely. This may indeed drive your discussion and provide peace of mind and **tens of thousands of dollars** in your pocket throughout your life.

As you prepare for retirement, consider this. YOU have EARNED a guaranteed pension that YOU cannot outlive. Historically your pension provides cost-of-living protection. You will have the option to receive a reduced monthly pension for **continuation** of your retirement pay should you predecease your spouse. This Survivor Benefit Plan, or SBP, is actually a form of lifetime term insurance on your life that allows you to continue providing a portion of this income stream even after your death.

Your decision to protect your pension boils down to risk management. The **risk** that you face is that when YOU die your pension will end and your spouse will have no income from this already-earned retirement income stream. You can fully **retain** this risk and, when you die, no one, including your spouse, will receive your monthly pension. You can fully **shift** this risk, paying maximum premiums into the Survivor Benefit Plan so that when you die your spouse will receive a portion of your pension. Or you can **share** this risk by partially enrolling in the SBP program to a minimal extent and then supplementing the remaining income stream with your own private insurance. As always, no matter WHICH risk management technique you select in the end, you will be better served having gone through this risk management thought process, analyzed your choices, and made the appropriate one for your family situation.

A closer look at your SBP program reveals some enticing attributes. In its simplest form, SBP is a lifetime term insurance policy paid with pre-tax premiums that requires no physical and no minimum health qualification. Thanks to the National Defense Authorization Act of 2004, there is no longer an offset with survivor Social Security payments after 2008. Should you choose to protect your pension with SBP, your premium is paid with pre-tax dollars. You will receive a reduced monthly pension amount reflective of your premium. Your health has no bearing on the premiums either. It is based on an average health formula reflective of military retiree health in previous years. Since it is a lifetime term policy, you MAY find cheaper insurance rates based on average health in the short term, but it's tough to beat in the long term. This being said, you NEED TO CONSIDER protecting your pension with a 35% SBP protection at a minimum for the reasons stated above.

What if your health isn't great when you retire? There is absolutely NO health-related physical associated with SBP, so this is the PREFERRED, 5-STAR choice for those of you in less-than-ideal health as a means to shift the risk of your pension protection.

What if you aren't married when you retire? What if you want to leave a stream of income to a **non-spouse**? What if you want to leave a **lump sum** RATHER than a stream of income to a spouse? What if you ONLY want to protect your retirement pay for a certain period of time, such as **25 years**? What if your spouse is significantly

OLDER than you are? What if you have additional assets or income streams and do not NEED to protect this stream of income for anyone? What if you want to leave a lump sum to **a church or a charity** when you die? Each of these cases leans towards alternative methods to **share** or **retain** the risk when protecting your pension.

The most common risk management alternative to the SBP, based on your feedback, is purchasing a private term life insurance contract. This assumes you are healthy enough to qualify, the underwriting life insurance company is financially strong, the death benefit is adequate to pay a desired amount to a survivor, and the timeframe covered reflects your desire to accept all risk after this policy expires. This method can provide cheaper premiums, although they are paid with after-tax dollars. It also allows you to control the beneficiary selection to allow non-spouses to receive the benefits after you die. Additionally, if your goal is to provide an asset (lump sum) rather than an income stream, then THIS method may be more appropriate for you. You can also select a lifetime term policy, if desired, to better reflect an alternative to SBP and eliminate your assumption of risk once the term expires. This represents a **financially viable alternative** for healthy pre-retirees, and deserves a serious look prior to retirement.

If you are leaning towards converting your pension to an asset rather than an income stream when you die, you may also wish to consider sharing your pension risk via a Variable Universal Life (VUL) insurance policy on your life. It's a very flexible way to ensure your family is taken care of after you pass from this earth. This is a form of permanent insurance, consisting of a term life insurance component and a tax-deferred investment component, which allows you to select mutual fund-type investments within your policy.

If you are **healthy** for your age there is a viable **alternative** to the SBP option that creates a legacy for your family. Think of it as a **benefit to you** for taking care of your health.

You are rewarded with a much lower premium if you are in good health. Part of each premium is invested in equities, which are historically higher returning vehicles over the long run than fixed rates of return. Now here's the best part of all: after a 20-year career, your retirement pay does **NOT** end at your death. By opting for a VUL instead of the SBP, **you will ALWAYS leave a financial legacy** unaffected by social security.

Here's an example for healthy pre-retirees.

Al and Vince are twin brothers who are both healthy 41 year-old Navy pre-retirees. Their younger brother Harry is a 40-year old Navy pre-retiree who will retire in one year. All are the same rank, and their retirement pay will be $1,600 monthly for the rest of their lives.

At retirement Al decides to accept the Survivor Benefit Plan (SBP), which guarantees that when he dies his spouse will receive an **income stream** of 55% of his retirement pay, or $880, for the rest of her life, with one exception. Should she remarry, her benefit can be suspended. The cost of this SBP is **$62** per month, paid with pre-tax premiums.

Vince decides to protect his pension by purchasing a Variable Universal Life (VUL) insurance policy instead. He will pay **$86** per month in after-tax premiums to insure his life for a **lump sum** of $320,000. The beneficiary is his spouse.

If Al dies the day after retirement, Al's wife receives $880 each month for the rest of her life, EXCEPT if she remarries (there's always a hooker on these policies). If Al's wife dies of grief **the day after Al dies**, then the rest of Al's family (brothers, sisters, nieces, nephews, etc) and his favorite charities (church, non-profit foundations) receive **no benefits** from the SBP for all of Al and his wife's efforts throughout his career. If both Al and his wife live for 50 more years, then he and his wife have paid **over $37,000** in total SBP payments, but neither Al, his wife, or their heirs received **any benefit at all**. This is an **expensive alternative** to protect the value of Al's retirement pay in the event of his early death.

Now let's suppose Vince dies the day after retirement. His spouse receives a $320,000 **asset** tax-free in death benefit from his policy. If she invests this in guaranteed Certificates of Deposit to earn 5%, and lives off of 4%, then she'll receive **at least** $1,200 monthly for the rest of her life...and meanwhile her principal **keeps growing!** It pays her whether she remarries or not. It provides partial inflation protection this way also because she's living off of less than she's earning, so in 10 years her 4% of principal is actually 4% of a much higher number.

If Vince's spouse dies the day after him, then their family or their favorite charities will receive $320,000 in benefits. So Vince and his wife **left a legacy to others** in return for their efforts throughout their career. Vince and his wife successfully transformed their military retirement benefit into a family legacy, continuing to provide income after they have both passed from this earth.

A year later, Harry and his wife decide to split the difference with Harry's retirement pension. He selects the 35% minimum SBP protection, paying $43 in pre-tax premiums to protect $560 in monthly payments. He also purchases a $150,000 25-yr term policy for $18 per month to protect the remaining portion of his retirement income. If Harry dies the day after he retires, his wife will receive $560 monthly from his SBP, and also received a check for $150,000. Assuming she invests this money in a CD and earns 5%, and then lives off of 4%, she can expect to receive on average $500 monthly in income. If Harry's wife dies the day after Harry died, then her beneficiaries receive the insurance proceeds, and this asset is passed on to loved ones after both Harry and his wife have died. They provided a financial legacy that will outlive both of them while still protecting his military pension income.

YOU have this choice. **YOU** can decide how **YOU** want to protect **your** retirement pension. However **YOU** decide to do so, you'll be better off having made an **informed decision** that best suits your needs.

Whatever you do, and this goes for all of your financial decisions, you are historically best served to follow the fundamental financial principles to **identify** your choices, **analyze** the pro's and con's of your options, **and take action!**

One additional area needs to be emphasized based on your feedback. You have the opportunity to select the minimum SBP, guaranteeing 35% of your pension income to your survivor rather than 55% commonly elected. This is the method Harry executed in our example. THEN you can certainly supplement your pension with a specified term or permanent private insurance policy to cover the remaining 20% of your pension amount for survivors, thereby SPREADING the risk between SBP and yourselves. **THIS REPRESENTS A PRUDENT APROACH TO PENSION PROTECTION FOR YOUR SURVIVORS**.

Action Item #15 is to CAREFULLY approach your pension protection. Get a quote from your SBP representative. Call a few term insurance companies to get quotes on coverage amounts. Use the rule of 4% risk-free rate of return to determine how much insurance coverage is appropriate to replace your stream of income if you died unexpectedly.

Action Item #16 is to consider a permanent form of insurance to replace a portion of your SBP if necessary. In this chapter we highlighted the decisions Al, Vince, and Harry made. It may be appropriate to consider permanent insurance, rather than term, to supplement your SBP coverage. Again, each case is different, as your health and goals affect the parameters of your decision. Gather your information, see how various alternatives compare, and make your choice that best fits your situation.

Chapter 13

Employment Benefits Decisions

Just suppose your boss walked up to you and said, "I like the work you're doing. However much you put into your savings account this year, I'm going to match it." How much would you put away?

Many, many bosses do just that, including federal, state, and county governments, but in a slightly different manner. It's referred to as 401(k) matching, or Thrift Savings Plan (TSP) match for civil service, or SIMPLE IRA matching, depending on the organization for which you work.

Funding your retirement plan during your working years is the main method of increasing your retirement standard of living. By offering to match your contributions (up to a limit), employers can **SIGNIFICANTLY** enhance your retirement lifestyle. **You just have to recognize it.**

By contributing to your retirement plan, you are electively foregoing current spending to set money aside for your future, and the Internal Revenue Service looks kindly on this. They offer a plethora of income tax incentives to businesses and individuals, including tax-deferral of gains, to entice you to help fund your own retirement. Your employer gets a nice tax deduction for matching your contribution, and gets a happy employee with a wonderful fringe benefit.

Whatever retirement plan your employer offers, whether it's a 401(k), Simplified Employee Pension-Individual Retirement Account (SEP-IRA), SIMPLE Individual Retirement Account (SIMPLE-IRA), a Tax Sheltered Annuity (TSA), or a Thrift Savings Plan (TSP), you should **always** discuss the pros and cons of it with your human resource personnel. Each plan affects different types and sizes of businesses and employees, and depending on whether your employer matches a portion of your contribution or not will greatly affect your standard of living in retirement.

If your goal is a comfortable retirement, then you've already decided to contribute a portion of each paycheck to your long-term goals. If your employer matches a portion of the money you set aside, then you should always contribute up to the **maximum** percentage **your employer matches**. In theory, it doesn't matter what the name on the retirement plan is – whether it's a federal Thrift Savings Plan or a private company 401k – you are receiving a tremendous benefit by contributing at least up to the **full matching level**.

Other typical benefits offered through your post-military employer include healthcare, dental, and vision benefits. Whether you are included in group healthcare policy or not, you always, as a military retiree, have access to Tri-Care. When you reach age 65, Tri-Care For Life offers a free benefit to supplement your Medicare coverage. Between retirement and age 65, you can always opt for Tri-Care Prime or Tri-Care Extended. Visit their website, **www.tricare.osd.mil** for additional information. Why is this important? If Tri-Care offers better coverage than your new employer's group health coverage, why not utilize it? You've qualified due to your military career. Why not compare it and use what's best for you? You've earned it!

Disability insurance coverage, both short and long-term, may be an important decision as well. You are protecting your ability to earn money. Were you to be disabled, even temporarily, such as with back surgery, a disability insurance policy can keep income flowing into your checkbook until you recover. Review pages 45 through 49 and revisit the need for disability insurance, then ask your HR department for costs.

Group life insurance may be available through your new job as well. Since you are no longer eligible for SGLI, you may want to compare rates at ReliaQuote.com as well as compare these against your group insurance rates. While group insurance may be cheaper now, you might have insurability issues later, so review your situation carefully. You might still wish to shift the insurance risk to your insurance company to replace your post-military retirement earnings should you die unexpectedly. Revisiting pages 45 through 49 will refresh your need and your decision to shift, share, or retain your life insurance risk.

Dental and vision health coverage are also options typically found through employer group health coverage. Make your decision based on how often you may or may not need coverage for these areas. Many veterans remarked that rather than pay premiums in these areas, they retained the risk, and identified former military dentists and opticians in their local communities. Rather than paying for insurance, your veterans paid with cash or credit cards on an **as-needed basis, at deep discounted prices.** They retained the risks, paid out of pocket for standard checkups, and rewarded themselves by keeping the premiums they otherwise would have paid in insurance costs. It's worth looking into through your employer.

Other areas to consider as you approach post-retirement employment include paid-for moving expenses and salary negotiations. Since you have a final move paid for by the military, employers may ask you to use this move to relocate to their city. That's up to you. Counter offer that in exchange for using your military move you'd like a sign-on bonus equal to at least half of the moving expense. In theory, it's cheaper for the hiring company to pay half the money to you as a bonus as it is to pay all of the money to move your family. Everything is negotiable!

On a similar note, when negotiating a salary, many veterans expressed dismay that employers would lowball them, knowing the retiree had a military pension coming in also. You know better; you realize that your value as an employee is based on what you earn for the company. It is independent of your military retirement pay. That should NEVER be a factor in a potential employer libeling you in salary negotiations. Put the ball back in their court by reminding them that your retirement pay is linked to your past underpayment and part of your overall compensation for life from the government for underpaying you during your career.

Action Item #17 is to ENSURE you take advantage of civilian employee retirement matching funds in whatever defined contribution plan your employer provides. Contribute at least up to the amount of the match; any contribution over that limit will be a pre-tax contribution to your qualified retirement plan, saving you federal income tax in the year of your contribution.

Action Item #18 is for you to identify whether or not you need disability, group life, dental, or vision insurance typically offered through your employer. Refer to pages 45 through 49, and ask questions specifically to your HR department at work.

Chapter 14

Real Estate, Income Taxes, and Unclaimed Property Searches

You (and other veterans) provided an ABUNDANCE of feedback regarding buying homes while active duty and whether to keep them as rentals or sell them when you move to your next duty station. Ironically, most Air Force personnel commented that they had built up quite a bit of equity in the home after apparently longer tours in one area, and were happy to cash out large profits tax-free by taking the $250,000 home profit exclusion ($500,000 for married filers) offered by our federal government. Marine Corps personnel, on the other hand, seemed reluctant to part with their homes in the northern Virginia area, especially the corridor from Quantico to Washington, DC. Their feedback focused on **renting their home** while they were relocated to their next duty station because at some point they felt they would return to that area on orders for another tour. Their concern, wise beyond their years, was that prices may NEVER go down to affordable levels again, so why not keep their rental now and **live in it upon their return** to that area on orders? ALL of these homeowners are correct in their logic. They reviewed their situations, looked at the pro's and con's of selling and renting, and

Regardless of your final decisions on selling versus renting your home when you move, remember to reference **IRS Publication 3, Armed Forces Tax Guide**, for recent income tax leniency. It's available online at irs.gov and has a wonderful search function to direct you expediently to your desired topic. Pub 3 has direct language explaining additional benefits extended to active duty service members, including **relaxed rules** when determining your tax-free profits after selling a former primary residence. **THIS KEEPS MONEY IN YOUR POCKET,** but you NEED to remain informed and updated, and this escapes tax preparation companies who don't focus on military personnel.

Further on the income tax issue, keep in mind that throughout your military career you will continuously need to file income taxes. Whether you buy a home, sell a home, rent it out, move, have children, get married, get divorced, or retire, you will ALWAYS be better served investing time to learn about income taxes. Armed Forces' Tax Guide, IRS Publication 3, is designed to assist you when preparing your income taxes. Be sure to **share it with your tax preparer** if you do not prepare your own taxes. This is a FREE publication designed to help you. If you had any shipmates or buddies killed during wartime, their widows NEED to consult this guide, as there are provisions in place for income tax relief.

Confusing? Then ask at your command if anyone can explain the following. President Bush signed into law the **Military Family Tax Relief Act of 2003** that included various provisions to help military personnel save federal income tax money. These include the following, listed directly as they appear on the irs.gov website.

1. Death benefits
The death gratuity paid to survivors of deceased Armed Forces members rises to $12,000 and is not taxable (was $6,000, with $3,000 tax-free). Effective for deaths occurring after 9/10/2001. Taxpayers amending a return to

use this provision should put "Military Family Tax Relief Act" in red in the top margin of Form 1040X.

2. Sale of principal residence

A taxpayer on qualified official extended duty in the U.S. Armed Services or the Foreign Service may suspend for up to 10 years of such duty time the running of the 5-year ownership-and-use period before the sale of a residence. This applies when the duty station is at least 50 miles from the residence – or while the person is residing under orders in government housing – for a period of more than 90 days or for an indefinite period. This election, which is an option for the taxpayer, applies to only one property at a time. Retroactive for home sales after May 6, 1997

3. Deduction for overnight travel expenses of National Guard and Reserve members

Reservists who stay overnight more than 100 miles away from home while in service (e.g., for a drill or meeting) may deduct unreimbursed travel expenses (transportation, meals and lodging) as an above-the-line deduction. The deduction is limited to the rates for such expenses authorized for federal employees, including per diem in lieu of subsistence.

4. Dept. of Defense Homeowners Assistance Program

Payments made after Nov. 11, 2003, under this program to offset the adverse effects on housing values of military base realignments or closures will be excludable from income as a fringe benefit.

5. Combat zone extensions expanded to contingency operations

The various extensions granted to combat zone participants to file returns or pay taxes will also apply to those serving in Contingency Operations, as designated by the Secretary of Defense. Effective for any acts whose deadline has not expired before Nov. 11, 2003.

6. Dependent care assistance programs
Clarifies that dependent care assistance programs for military personnel are excludable benefits. Effective for tax years after 2002.

7. Military academy attendees
The ten percent tax on payments from a Qualified Tuition Program or Coverdell Education Savings Account that are not used for educational expenses does not apply to attendees of the U.S. Military, Naval, Air Force, Coast Guard or Merchant Marine Academies, to the extent the payments do not exceed the costs of advanced education. Effective for tax years after 2002.

Each of the above tax provisions provides incentives to keep money in your pocket. Even if they don't apply directly to you or your current situation, they may be applicable to a known airman, shipmate, soldier, or fellow co-worker. Be aware that they are located and updated at irs.gov, and always available as a reference.

Many veterans were **less concerned** with education funding than could be expected. There are 3 reasons provided for this position. First, there are a PLETHORA of military education grants and financial aid packages available to military personnel, so be sure and utilize these funds. Second, the military itself provides the FINEST form of education, which is **a paid On the Job Training program** right out of high school. If you can find a better education program for 18-year olds than enlisting in our military, then e-mail us. Third, on limited military pay, funds earmarked SPECIFICALLY for education, such as Coverdell Savings Accounts and 529 plans, may be penalized with 10% penalties and income tax consequences if NOT used for QUALIFIED education purposes. This actually discourages some investments from being tagged for these programs.

Briefly, because it was not top priority from your feedback, here are some considerations for your own situation. If you want to fund a child's private parochial schooling, such as private Catholic high school, then invest in a Coverdell Savings Account, which can be used for parochial education. If you earmark money for college education, regardless of WHERE your child might someday attend, then visit **www.SavingForCollege.com**, and pay CLOSE attention to the **Utah direct investor plan**. It has low expenses, fine underlying investments, and provides tremendous value when compared to other plans. It also provides all types of discussion regarding the pro's and con's of 529 plans in general.

By this point in your career you've changed banks, investment companies, states, and perhaps countries. It's a wonderful time to take a moment and search online, for free, to see if anyone owes you anything for any accounts you've had along the way.

What we mean by this is search for any unclaimed property in your name, your spouse's name, your parents' names, and any children's names also. Visit the free website **www unclaimed.org** and then select any state in which you've resided. Search by name, and by social security number to be certain. Search also by any business names you or your spouse used during your careers. Banks, investment companies, insurance companies, and even the IRS may have refunds awaiting your claim. After a certain period of time, these financial institutions return this unclaimed money to their state treasury, which advertises periodically via newspaper and internet in attempts to find the rightful owners. It costs nothing and potentially can reward you with found money. Now THAT'S a great investment in time. Before you search, consider REMINDING yourself of the Rule of 1/3, and applying it appropriately to any "found money" you run across. We extend our special thanks to Melinda in Williamsburg, for sharing this potentially lucrative reminder. Happy hunting!

Action Item #19 is to visit www.unclaimed.org and search for any unclaimed property held by states in which you formerly resided.

Action Item #20 is to visit and review the informative website, www.SavingForCollege.com, for college education savings and investments. This site explains 529 plans and offers plan comparisons for you. This is a terrific resource to share with friends also.

Action Item #21 is to call the IRS at 1-800-829-1040 or visit the website **www.irs.gov** to order a free copy of Publication 3, the Armed Forces Tax Guide. This publication can be shared with your income tax preparer to save you additional money when you file income taxes.

Section 4

ARRIVAL
Post-Military Finances and Planning For
Your Survivor Spouse

Review and update these documents:
1. Wills, POAs, Emergency Data Sheet
2. Beneficiaries on SGLI life insurance, Thrift Savings Plan, and Roth IRA accounts
3. Titling on house, autos, boats
4. Beneficiaries on all life insurance, retirement plan, and Payable On Death (POD)/Transfer On Death (TOD) accounts

Consider these 4 discussions:
1. Estate management continuity
2. Cashflow versus Asset conversion
3. Retirement communities versus Home Health Care
4. Gifting assets to heirs while alive

Read these 3 books from your local library:
1. Beating the Street by Peter Lynch
2. The Intelligent Investor by Benjamin Graham, forward by Warren Buffet
3. AARP Crash Course in Estate Planning by Michael Palermo

Chapter 15

Post-Retirement Cashflow and Inflation

There are two huge 'speed bumps' regarding your full retirement finances. You get to plan for these and there are various "work-arounds" to keep them in check. Just be aware that they are your two main financial opponents during retirement. These hindrances are **inflation** and **income taxes**.

Inflation, as you well know, is the erosion of purchasing power. For instance, to mail a letter in 1970 cost 8 cents for a stamp. Today it costs 37 cents. The average home in 1970 was $16,500. Today it costs $134,000. Let's say you had a shipmate named Mick who buried a shoebox containing $16,500 in his backyard in 1970, and dug it up in 2002, his $16,500 would **not buy** an average home. (Actually, it would barely buy a car for him these days!) That is the effect of inflation on your long-term investments. This is a hurdle you need to overcome to ensure the money you invest for the future grows at a rate higher than inflation.

Income taxes **act as an anchor** on your long-term investing because they are, in effect, an added cost. For instance, Danny deposited $10,000 in a 1-year Certificate of Deposit paying 3%. One year later, his account value was $10,300, and he received a Form 1099 –INT from his bank for $300 of earned interest. This statement means he will pay additional tax for his earnings when he files his federal tax return in April. For example, if **you** invested $1,000 and earned 10% in just 10 months, then you have a total value of $1,100. But you will pay tax on the 10% gain, so paying the tax out of the same account at the 28% rate leaves a $1,072 balance. Can you now see how **taxes** decrease your investments? Any added expense, such as taxes, **reduces your investment return** and thus slows down your pursuit of your financial goals. This is ESPECIALLY important in retirement.

Here is a quick example of a guaranteed safe, FDIC-insured Certificate of Deposit that you can buy at your bank next door to show the effects of our first two speed bumps:

Jan 1, 2005: You place **$100,000** in a 1-year Certificate of Deposit earning 1.5% interest.

Dec 31, 2005: Account totals **$101,500**.

So, you as an investor are ahead $1,500 (or 1.5%) for investing in a safe, guaranteed investment, correct? Therefore you have 1.5% more purchasing power than last year, correct? **Not so fast, my friend.** You have to pay **income taxes** on that earned interest. Even if you are in the 15% tax bracket, which is quite rare if you are drawing a military retirement pension and social security, you'll owe $225 on that $1,500 in earnings. So your after-tax gain is actually **$1,275**, meaning your total account value after paying taxes is **$101,275**. It would be EVEN LOWER had you been in the next higher federal income tax bracket, 25%, OR paid state income taxes on this money.

However, if the **cost-of-living**, as inflation is commonly referred to, increased 3% that year, then we also need to factor this in. **Inflation**, unfortunately, **attacks both the earnings and the principal.** In fact, Jim, a former Army pilot, refers to inflation as **"the Silent Thief."** So we

Army pilot, refers to inflation as **"the Silent Thief."** So we must lower our entire $101,275 account value by 3% to properly account for inflation, which rounded off is $3,038. So our net buying power, after inflation and taxes, is thus $98,237. **You actually lost purchasing power** by keeping money in a short-term CD **after accounting for taxes and inflation!**

This isn't the end of the world, however. There are 3 historically prudent techniques to offset the detrimental effects of inflation and taxes using guaranteed principal-protection products. If you like your investment principal guaranteed, meaning the initial investment never declines in value, your tradeoff may be to purchase longer-term CDs, medium term government bonds, and medium term fixed annuities. CDs are guaranteed through the Federal Deposit Insurance Corporation, federal government bonds are backed by the full faith and credit of our federal government (they print money!), and fixed annuities by the financial strength of the underwriting insurance company.

While our 1-yr CD paid just 1.5% at the time of this writing, a 2-yr CD pays 2.5%, a 3-year CD pays 3.0%, a 4-yr CD pays 3.5%, and a 5-yr CD pays 4.0%. The longer you agree to tie up your money the higher the interest rate the bank offers.

So let's revisit your $100,000 investment in a CD from last page. What if you put $20,000 into each of the 5 CDs from the previous paragraph, with varying terms from 1 to 5 years? Here are the corresponding earnings from your CDs:

Amount invested	Interest rate	Interest Earned
$20,000	1.5%	$ 300
$20,000	2.5%	$ 500
$20,000	3.0%	$ 600
$20,000	4.0%	$ 800
$20,000	5.0%	$1,000

If you KNOW you will keep these monies invested, and you plan on living off just the interest, then purchasing a CD-ladder represents a prudent approach to protect your principal while earning an **overall higher** average rate of return on your money. As the one-year CD comes due, simply buy a 5-year CD with the principal. Each of your other CDs are now 1 year closer to coming due!

Your risks associated with investing 100% of your capital this way include inflation and interest rate risk. On the plus side, your principal never fluctuates in value, your principal is guaranteed by FDIC, and your investment only **increases** in value. On the down side, all of your interest earned will be taxed at your ordinary federal tax rates, whether you use it or reinvest it, you are susceptible to inflation, and you typically pay a penalty if you need to break the CD to your principal prior to the end of the term. Other than keeping al of your principal buried in your yard or deposed in a savings account, this is the most conservative approach to protecting your investments in retirement.

Even less conservative is the federal government bond approach. Let's use your same $100,000 to invest in government bonds and compare your risks and returns to your CDs. When you buy a bond you are loaning your principal to the bond issuer in exchange for interest paid on your money for a specified length of time. At the end of the bond term you can expect to receive your entire principal back. A 3-year bond issued by the U.S. Treasury currently pays 3.1%. A 5-year bond pays 4.0%. As the length of the term increases, the interest rate typically (but not always) increases, similar to CDs. There is a major difference when investing in bonds, however. Although your principal is still guaranteed by the government, it may **FLUCTUATE in value** based on interest rate changes. A bond held to term will still return the entire principal, but a bond sold prior to term **may be sold for more or less than its original purchase price**. Here's why.

Tina paid $10,000 for a 10-year, 8% U.S. Treasury bond on January 1, 2000. She received 8% per year, or $800, in interest, expecting to receive her entire $10,000 principal back when her bond comes due on January 1, 2010. She decided to cash out her bond early on January 1, 2005, when new U.S. Treasury 10-year bonds are paying 6% interest. Can Tina expect to receive her full $10,000 back? Did her principal fluctuate in value? Will she receive a premium or a discount on her $10,000 when she sells her bond early?

The good news is Tina received a premium when she sold her bond early. Since current market rates are LOWER than the rate on her bond, prudent investors will pay MORE, known as a premium, to have the higher income stream that her bond will continue to pay for another 5 years. While the federal government guaranteed Tina's principal IF HELD TO TERM, the principal value FLUCTUATED based on interest rate movements during the time she held her bond. Had Tina invested in a CD instead of a bond, she would have SHIFTED the fluctuating principal risk to the issuing bank rather than RETAINED that risk by holding a bond. This is an **important concept to remember** when comparing guaranteed principal products for your investments. Whether you accept fluctuating principal or not is up to YOU based on YOUR risk tolerances and YOUR financial goals.

The third type of guaranteed principal investment is a fixed annuity, where the guaranteeing source is the financial strength of the underwriting insurance company. While there are varying types of annuities, including deferred, immediate, and variable, for this discussion we will strictly focus on the deferred fixed annuity. These act similar to CDs, as you invest a lump sum, receive a fixed interest rate, and collect your principal in full at the end of the term.

With a fixed deferred annuity your principal is still guaranteed, your principal does not fluctuate in value, and overall account value only goes up as interest is credited over time. On the plus side, you have more control over income taxes with a deferred annuity than with a CD because you are **not taxed** on the interest earned UNTIL YOU WITHDRAW IT. Once you do draw from the account, your interest is always assumed to be paid first, and will be taxed at ordinary tax rates with no special capital gains treatment. In essence, you are loaning a lump sum to the insurance company in exchange for a fixed rate of interest for a certain period, and then you can collect your principal again. You have SHIFTED all investment risk to the insurance company, but you retain the inflation risk in doing so.

For comparison purposes, two sisters, Debbie and Lindy, plan to invest $100,000 each into a guaranteed principal investment for 5 years. Lindy selects a 5-year FDIC-insured bank CD paying 5%, and Debbie invests $100,000 into a 5-year deferred fixed annuity paying 4.5% with a financially strong insurance company. Both are in the 25% federal tax bracket. The only time either sister can withdraw from the account, without penalty, is to pay income taxes due in that year on the earnings from that account. Who has the higher account value at the end of 5 years given these conditions?

It might seem like an unfair question, as Lindy earns 5% on her money and Debbie only earns 4.5% on her investment and both start out with the same amount. Both invest in guaranteed investments where the principal does not fluctuate. Both have shifted market risk to the underwriting institutions, and neither investment will ever go down in value. So who, given these parameters, ends up with more?

It's Debbie by a nose! But why?

Remember that Lindy's investment of choice, a 5-year CD, triggers income taxes on earnings **every year**, whether the interest is withdrawn or reinvested. For our example we specified that taxes incurred needed payment from that account. Lindy's effective interest earned was 5%, but she only keeps 75% of that interest rate as she loses 25% to income taxes, equating to a net 3.75% annual AFTER TAX effective interest rate. Lindy's $100,000 investment grew to **$120,210.**

Debbie's fixed deferred annuity investment triggers taxable earned income ONLY WHEN WITHDRAWN. So Debbie's 4.5% earned interest rate is effective until the money is withdrawn, when her 25% income tax comes due. Debbie's money compounded faster because she did not pay taxes on it annually. Debbie's $100,000 grew to $127,628 in 5 years earning 4.5% annually. Debbie owes $6,908 in taxes, representing 25% of her $27,628 earned interest. Debbie wound up with a total account value in 5 years of **$120,720.**

This is a very common yet OUTSTANDING example of why YOU need to understand YOUR goals, YOUR plans for when and why to invest your money, and how **different types of investments** affect YOUR bottom line.

Going one step further, some of you wrote in asking about "combination annuity" techniques. This is an income tax efficient means of providing current income while maintaining the semblance of a fixed principal investment, but should be JUDICIOUSLY APPLIED when used, and sparingly at that. Here's how it works.

June's husband passed away, leaving her with reduced monthly income from social security and Survivor

Benefit plan. She has $300,000 in life insurance proceeds but is not an experienced investor. She wants to simplify her life and enhance her monthly cashflow, but doesn't want to spend a lot of time on investments nor take much risk with this money.

Rather than invest in a 5-year CD or a 5-year deferred annuity, as Debbie and Lindy did in our previous example, June wants more income than these products can provide. She finds that a combination annuity fits her needs. She invests $254,000 into a deferred fixed annuity, guaranteed to grow back to $300,000 in 5 years. She invests the remaining $46,000 into an immediate annuity for 5 years, meaning she'll be paid $937 each month with this money, part in interest and part in principal, until it is depleted. It's OK to deplete this portion, by design, since she knows her deferred fixed annuity is designed to grow back to her original amount, $300,000. Then she can repeat this on one more occasion if she'd like, depending on interest rates in the future.

This represents a more tax efficient means for June to receive income, as a portion of each immediate annuity payment is a return of capital, hence it is not taxed. This will LOWER June's federal income tax bill, keeping more money in her pocket. Beware of the hidden tax burden after the initial timeframe, as now her $300,000 mature deferred annuity contains almost 18% in gains, which will be taxable when June starts withdrawing it. This technique is most efficient when used for two full cycles, so you may want to investigate using 7-year or 10-year cycles to lengthen and broaden your overall tax savings.

One last type of annuity, an Equity Index Annuity, remains high on your list of investments to consider. These represent the most widely **OVERSOLD** investment by major banks and brokers. The underlying premise is that you have downside protection in the form of a guaranteed

MINIMUM investment return on your money, yet you can reasonable expect a higher average return by participating in a portion of the higher returns historically of the index to which it is linked. For example, the most common EIAs guarantee 3% annually with the potential to share in upside profits up to 10% each year, where a cap is in place to stop your gains. These are typically VERY LUCRATIVE for the sales associate mentioning them. They contain above average internal costs to administer. They are a relatively new type of annuity, sold by insurance companies, which should be limited to a small portion of your portfolio in most cases and not used while still building your wealth.

Just to summarize this section, a single **short-term** CD is intended to be a safe, secure place to keep short-term money. A **CD ladder**, where portions of your investments are spread out among longer timeframes in equal amounts, represents an alternative method to help stay ahead of inflation. A CD ladder also still provides the safety and **guarantee** of a fixed principal investment.

Fixed flexible annuities also represent alternative methods to outpace inflation, as your principal is still **guaranteed**, this time by the financial strength of the underwriting insurance company. As interest rates rise, you historically capture a portion of these increases through higher interest credited to your account. Be careful, as always, in selecting proper companies to back your annuity investments, as your principal is ONLY guaranteed by that company's financial strength. In other words, choose a STRONG one!

Similar to fixed flexible annuities are flexible CDs. These are still FDIC-insured instruments, but in rising interest rate environments they become popular. Flexible CDs allow you to lock in a higher interest rate one time during your CD term. If interest rates rise after a year, you have the opportunity to lock in the higher rate at that time for the remainder of your CD term. These can be terrific for peace of mind and also allow you to partially offset interest rate risk associated with longer term CDs. **Consider these instruments** when CD shopping.

Also take note of how combination annuity approaches can soften your tax burden and keep more money in your pocket. Be sure and get two quotes on these investments, as the timeframes involved and rates of return can swing wildly as you move from 5-year to 10-year timeframes for these cycles.

Finally, use extreme caution if a sales person mentions Equity Index Annuities as a "great way to build wealth", for they are probably referring to their own commissions rather than building YOUR wealth. They can be used to protect a portion of your wealth once built, but should not make up too much of your overall portfolio in general. Watch New York attorney general Elliot Spitzer's case against two very large insurance companies during the next few years to see why these indeed appear very oversold and used for the wrong purposes. This opinion results directly from veterans who have experienced the pain of these investments that were oversold, overpromised and, not surprisingly, underdelivered.

Action Item #22 invites you to review your current holdings, paying special attention to the effects of inflation and income taxes. Is your current portfolio more similar to a bond ladder or have you lessened the effects of income taxes by deferring them with annuities? Are you considering the use of annuities, and if so, WHERE are you getting an unbiased second opinion? It may well be worth a few hundred dollars to get a second opinion from a fee-only planner before purchasing any annuities just in case, unless you are experienced and they are from a solid, trustworthy insurance company.

Action item #23 requests you to project the effects of inflation on the fixed income portion of your portfolio by calculating the average interest rate earned overall. Is it higher or lower than the historical 3.4% inflation rate? Are you staying ahead of inflation? This is a solid time to double-check prior to finding out the hard way years from now, when your dollars buy less purchasing power.

Chapter 16

Becoming More Financially Conservative in Retirement

In their feedback, military retirees also recommended emphasizing the typical risk tolerance shift towards more conservative investing in retirement. Retirees with great intentions **know** they need some financial and estate planning assistance, listen attentively to a plan on how to achieve their goals, and then **hesitate to follow through** on taking action to get started. They never give themselves a chance to succeed. By waiting until they find that perfect investment, they **rob themselves** of time reallocated more conservatively in the stock markets, and that's time that cannot be made up.

After you have successfully accumulated money for your retirement, you may wish to shift from a **"let's grow our money"** mindset to a **"let's protect our money"** state of mind. This is typically reflected in two facets of a couple's finances, **risk tolerance and spending habits**, and emphasized even heavier after the passing of the first spouse. This is EXTREMELY COMMON, as well as EXTREMELY PRUDENT, so if you already have passed through this phase in life feel welcome to pass along your experiences on this subject.

It is natural for our risk tolerances to decline once we reach full retirement. WHY do you need to accept the risk of growing your investments when you've already built them up to levels you like? You have already assumed the risk associated with growing your investments. At this time it is certainly appropriate, if you wish, to **decrease** your risk, thus protecting your investments, with the tradeoff of growth no longer needed for your entire portfolio. After completing the earned income portion of your life you now rely mainly on pensions and investments for income. There is no longer a steady stream of paychecks deposited in your checking account every two weeks to replenish your spending.

Given this outlook, **do you have enough income**? From where should you take money to replace an automobile? How much should you keep in your emergency account now? Should you pay off your mortgage if you can? What percentage of your investment portfolio should be in bonds? How much in stocks? How much in bank Certificate of Deposits? YOU can arrive at the answers to these questions and more by asking YOURSELVES what your true goals are.

Basically, **HOW MUCH** monthly income do you want? How much income can you count on EACH MONTH for the rest of your lives from your investments? You may have earned a military pension, a government pension, a private industry pension, a non-profit pension, a teacher's pension, and qualified for Social Security pension, or some combination of these common pensions. Perhaps you also built up large 401k, IRA, or non-retirement investment accounts through the years also. At some point sound financial principals dictate a need to determine WHERE your monthly income is coming from, HOW MUCH you wish to take, HOW MUCH RISK is involved, if any, in the monthly amount fluctuating, and HOW GUARANTEED PRINCIPAL you want while protecting your investments.

Now that you've decided HOW MUCH income you want each month, IDENTIFIED the sources to provide it, and you have your income streams set up, it's time to consider simplifying and consolidating. As the old saying goes, "Tomorrow is promised to no one."

Action Item #24 is to recalculate your risk tolerance for your investments. If you trade online, you have access to risk tolerance tools online. If you have a broker, or use a financial planner, ask for their assistance. It's important to calculate your risk tolerances for you and your spouse separately, indicating who is more conservative among you (as if you didn't already know). Becoming more conservative in retirement is common, as you shift from growing to protecting.

Chapter 17

Contingency Planning As Your Final Act of Love

Today's major financial services companies have responded remarkably quickly to consumer demand for simplification and consolidation. Whether your primary brokerage account is, as many of you indicated in your feedback, with Scottrade, Fidelity, USAA, or Vanguard, you are able to buy, sell, and trade a plethora of non-proprietary mutual funds, stocks, bonds, and brokered CDs at one brokerage. This simplifies YOUR financial life – you can still diversify your investments by holding Fidelity funds, Vanguard index funds, USAA bond funds, Exxon-Mobil stock, a $50,000 CD, and IBM bonds, and they will all be consolidated on one statement. You can link a checkbook to your brokerage account, providing liquidity at your fingertips. You can track, trade, and research from one site. This represents a time-saving, secure method that benefits wise consumers tremendously.

There is an additional benefit to consolidating as well. Now may be the time to review your investments, reward yourself by replacing your contractual plans and load mutual funds that are underperforming with more efficient no-load mutual funds, and minimizing market fluctuations by locking in fixed principal investments. When the time comes, your surviving spouse will have one company to contact regarding investments. If your surviving spouse is the primary money handler and bill payer already, this makes life easy. If not, your surviving spouse has a company that YOU trusted handling the assets, and can typically receive MUCH BETTER ADVICE after your death because of your consolidation. DO NOT OVERLOOK the benefit of ACCOUNTABILITY to your loved ones when consolidating. YOU are providing continuity through investments. YOU are providing continuity for money management. YOU are providing continuity for income streams, sound financial advice, proper investments, and trust through your affiliation with a consolidated investment account. CHOOSE WELL.

One sideline to the facet of accountability through consolidation is offered from numerous veteran SURVIVING SPOUSES. They received outstanding assistance from military organizations, including Department of Defense, Veterans Administration, Veterans of Foreign Wars, Tri-Care, and the American Legion regarding funeral services, Survivor Benefit pay, military benefits, and Tri-Care for Life health insurance. Yet most felt relatively helpless with finances if their spouse was the primary moneyhandler and investor. They didn't know where to turn for ongoing assistance with investments. Unfortunately, many were guided into less-than-stellar, above-average risk products at local banks. While this was great for bank profits, it was NOT in the best interests, looking back with 20/20 vision, for the surviving spouses. **What lessons were learned from their mistakes**, and what can YOU do to prepare going forward?

First, you don't need to push your spouse into a crash course in finances and investing at this stage in life. Second, you do need to identify trustworthy financial institutions to delegate your investment duties should you die first. This is your "Act of Love" for your survivors. For extra credit, consider having this trusted financial institution prepare a Survivor Financial Plan of some type prior to your death so that YOU can help formulate the foundation for your survivor. This simple method provided a SIGNIFICANT amount of confidence in both spouses, knowing there is a contingency financial plan in place, and represents good headwork.

As part of your contingency financial plan, first consider cashflow, then decide whether your spouse's risk tolerance will change. Your military retirement will stop, and the SBP payment will begin. How much life insurance is in place? What other assets will be affected by your death (other pensions, social security, deferred compensation plans)? Rather than receiving BOTH social security checks, your surviving spouse will only receive the higher of the two. When will assets, such as automobiles, need to be replaced? Is that accounted for in your plan? If your spouse is less risk tolerant, how much can your spouse expect by investing more conservatively? If there is a mortgage remaining, should you it be paid off after your death if your spouse is risk averse?

These are vital questions that MAY as well be addressed prior to your death. They are PERSONAL in nature, and will have EMOTIONAL as well as financial components when analyzed. Be aware of this, because what makes logical sense to you MAY NOT be comfortable to your survivor.

For example, assume it is now 2009. Elvis and Kathy are a married couple, each 85 years old, with $400,000 in bond mutual funds and $100,000 in equity mutual funds that Elvis manages. They draw $2,000 monthly from Elvis's social security, $2,000 monthly from Kathy's social security, and $2,500 monthly from Elvis's Army pension. They own a home worth $300,000 and owe $100,000 on a mortgage with 10 years remaining at 6% interest. Elvis is the primary investor for the family, and

Kathy takes care of monthly budgets and bill paying. Elvis reads this book (please excuse the shameless self-promotion), recognizes how this situation fits his family, and picks up the phone to call Acme Investing (apologies to Wile E. Coyote) to ask for a Contingency Financial Plan review with their long-time financial advisor Don.

Here's how Don properly addresses their concerns. If Elvis dies, how does Kathy's cashflow change? Elvis's social security will STOP, as Kathy makes the identical amount on her own accord; otherwise she would get the step-up to the higher of the two, and drop the lower. Kathy will receive $2,000 monthly from social security. Elvis's Army pension will be **diminished**, and Kathy will receive 35% of his former $2,500 monthly pension, resulting in $875 of monthly income. Her military survivor pension will increase annually for cost of living allowances, as does her social security. That's it for monthly income. Their mortgage payment remains the same. The monthly money flowing into their checking account each month **DROPPED from $6,500 monthly to $2,875** after Elvis's death. True, monthly expenses will decrease, such as only one automobile to operate and lower food bills, but the DROP IN EXPENSES is **much less than** the DROP IN INCOME.

This has historically been a real problem after the primary moneyhandler dies. At this point, the non-moneyhandler spouse is faced with **unfamiliar** investment decisions, and is statistically MORE LIKELY to want less risk for his or her investments. Peruse the nasd.com website and you'll find higher rates of surviving spouses being misled by financial advisors. YOU CAN PREVENT THIS FROM HAPPENING TO YOUR SPOUSE. You can take action NOW, review your "what if" scenario PRIOR to your death, delegate a trusted financial institution as a back-up investment handler, and sleep well knowing you have a contingency financial plan in place just in case.

Don then asks Kathy a about her comfort with investments, and she is worried. She is MUCH less comfortable with the stock market fluctuations if Elvis is not monitoring their investments, and indicates to Don that she would prefer to have NO MORE THAN 20%of her remaining investment assets fluctuating in principal. She prefers the other 80% be invested in guaranteed principal investments too, just to make sure she doesn't lose money. As is common, Kathy chooses to protect her investments even more. After Elvis's death, she sees a reduced monthly income, high monthly mortgage, and is less comfortable with fluctuating stock market prices. Since Kathy will still be in the 25% federal income tax bracket, and is even more conservative in her risk tolerance for investments, let's look at her options.

Option 1 will be to mainly keep doing what they were doing as a couple. She can keep paying on her mortgage, reallocate her investments with Don to be 40% in FDIC-insured CDs and 40% in fixed annuities, with the remaining 20% in a moderate, balanced mutual fund allocation. Her cashflow will be much tighter than she's used to, but she can expect to live from all of the income generated by her fixed portfolio if she wishes.

Option 2 will be to pay off her mortgage. The math breaks down this way. When she pays $1 in interest on her mortgage, at the end of the year the federal government credits her back 25 cents of that money in the form of reduced federal income taxes. That's it. She still spent 75 cents of that dollar on interest payment to a financial institution. Since her mortgage rate is 6%, her effective AFTER-TAX interest rate is 4.5%. That's how much, after factoring in her tax credit, she is paying in interest on her mortgage. If she pays 4.5% after-tax TO a financial institution in interest (her mortgage payments), but receives only 3% interest pre-tax FROM a financial institution in interest (her CD investments), **she is losing ground** with her money. She is paddling upstream. If she can BEAT that 4.5% interest rate with her after-tax investment returns, then she comes out ahead by keeping the mortgage and investing her money. If she can't beat that rate, then it makes sense to just pay off her mortgage. It's the equivalent, more or less, of finding an investment paying 4.5% after-tax each year. That's a tough number to beat in 2006, especially given her conservative risk tolerance.

Again, this decision is part emotional as well. If she chooses, she can pay off the mortgage with part of her guaranteed principal investments, effectively locking in a 4.5% after-tax rate of return. Then she will see a greater monthly disposable cashflow resulting from no mortgage payment outflow each month. She can choose at that time to reinvest all or a portion of this higher monthly income if she wishes to replenish her investments with which she paid off her mortgage. Don clearly lays out these options to Elvis and Kathy, and Kathy leans towards this option. Elvis completely understands, and essentially this portion of their contingency planning is complete.

As you know from ALL military planning, **a plan is merely a point from which to deviate.** Don explains that depending on market conditions down the road Kathy may be able to invest in a 3-year CD and receive 8% interest, which translates to 6% after-tax rate of return assuming she remains in the 25% federal tax bracket. If this happens, she is wise to keep the mortgage in place, as this beats her 4.5% after-tax rate of return. Understanding there is an emotional component again to this decision, if Kathy chooses to have no mortgage and a higher monthly disposable income (no mortgage payment), then that is HER choice also. She has a lot of flexibility built in, and now understands the underlying concept better than ever.

At this point, Don would review the same scenarios, including cashflow and investments, with Elvis assuming Kathy predeceases him. Also part of contingency planning is reviewing wills, trusts (if applicable), powers of attorney, long-term healthcare planning, and perhaps gifting of assets while they are alive if they so choose.

Elvis and Kathy have enough life experience to realize they can save a lot of money by investing their own **time, knowledge, and desire** to better understand contingency planning. There are books available, tapes, seminars, and a plethora of information available on the internet. Most (if not all) military affiliated organizations offer free information regarding these topics. IF they want to pay for an unbiased second opinion, they can get it. It's THEIR choice, which is an empowering feeling at any stage of life.

Also worth mentioning is the "what if" scenario revolving around long-term illnesses. What if Kathy were to become ill? How would they pay for nursing home care? This goes back to risk again, and they can retain it, shift it, or share it. Retaining the risk of one (or both) becoming ill translates to paying for it with cashflow and investments. Shifting it means full **long-term healthcare insurance**, paying premiums in exchange for shifting the risk to pay for care. Sharing it means partial healthcare insurance while retaining a portion of the costs themselves. Some people prefer to pay with their own assets, others prefer to shift the risk to protect their assets to pass to future generations. This is THEIR choice, and up to them to decide how they wish to approach this "what if" scenario.

After reviewing Kathy and Elvis's estate planning, Don recommends one enhancement. He suggests using Payable On Death (POD) account titling for checking, savings, and CD accounts by the surviving spouse. He also recommends Transfer On Death (TOD) account titling for mutual fund holdings after the first spouse dies. His reasoning is simple. After the first spouse dies, the remaining spouse still needs to maintain control over accounts, yet simplify the transfer of asset after the second spouse passes. This can be accomplished with POD and TOD titling.

POD titling is accomplished using a free form, available at most if not all major banks, and it enables the account owner to name beneficiaries for that account. Upon the death of the sole account owner, the account AUTOMATICALLY, and without probate, passes to the designated beneficiary AND AVOIDS PROBATE. Don reminds Kathy and Elvis that, when the time comes, they may want to revisit this idea, to ensure their assets pass directly to their heirs to avoid probate, and Kathy and Elvis nod in agreement. Don has mentioned an idea that, when the time comes, can be used properly because it has been pre-approved by Kathy and Elvis prior to being needed. THIS is an added benefit of continuation planning.

You may wish to revisit your continuation planning in anther light. What if the primary investor in the family is incapacitated? What if both spouses are less interested in keeping up with investments as they age? The need for continuity for your investments is essential. You may wish to establish your backup now, while you are in good health and spirits. As demand for contingency financial planning increases, more financial institutions and brokerages are beefing up their trust departments. You can save a LOT of time and money by pricing a few different companies and asking for written proposals. By interviewing and picking a trusted company to advise you now, you can delegate this daily responsibility to them while healthy and monitor their approach to keep them in check. Then it becomes a simple transition when incapacitation or death comes to visit. This is also vital if you are leaving money to non-moneyhandler children or minors. Choose wisely.

Now that you've built this wealth, **you have three options** on how to pass it along after you've passed from this earth. It can go to your heirs, your favorite charity, or to pay estate and transfer taxes. You have total control over any of these three options, but if **you** don't decide then the government will decide for you by existing death tax law.

Most commonly, people leave as much as possible to heirs, but more and more people are arranging trusts to attain maximum control after they've died. Trusts offer tremendous benefits to loved ones and to society. Here are two quick examples.

To ensure your children from a previous marriage are not cut out of your will, you can have money placed in a trust. The income generated from the trust's assets can pay for your spouse's maintenance, but when your spouse dies the remaining assets (or a portion thereof) go directly to your children from a previous marriage.

A second common use of trusts is the creation of the Private Family Foundation, which can qualify as a charity with your children involved in providing grants to causes you supported while alive. This is a tremendous means of passing along money management skills while additionally passing along the money that you created during your lifetime.

Both of these examples touch on the subject of estate planning. More importantly, these examples show a need for planning after your own death, to ensure that your assets are dispersed at your direction and with your intentions. They represent your **Final Act of Love**, which you design, control, and to some extent implement through your choice of executor.

Action Item #25 is to consider simplifying and consolidating your investments. Which company has the statements you prefer? Which company can hold the types of assets you wish to invest in? Which companies offer a range of financial products so that you can get opinions on all investments, including mutual funds, stocks, bonds, annuities, and CDs, with one phone call? The final decision is yours, but many veterans cite time and energy tracking investments as two reasons to consolidate.

Action Item #26 is to go through your portfolio with "what if" questions regarding first your own death and then the death of your spouse. Would there be enough cashflow? Which pension cashflows would be reduced? Have you adequately replaced income cashflow with insurance benefits if you chose that route? Just ensure your cashflow is adequate in the event of a spousal death or incapacitation of either of you.

Action Item #27 is to review your current account titling to see if POD or TOD is more proper. How much of your assets will be depleted if they pass through probate? Are you unintentionally creating paperwork and worry for your survivors if you keep account titling as it is now? How can you retitle to more accurately reflect your desires yet maintain control of your accounts?

Epilogue

To summarize the input from veterans, the common theme in achieving any financial goal is paying yourself first, then living on less than you earn, investing to stay ahead of inflation, and passing along your financial skills and wealth to others. These fundamentals remain essential, even in retirement. It's a simple yet very effective recipe for accumulating AND PROTECTING wealth in a free market society.

Managing money is a learned skill, not a birthright. No doctor in a delivery room says, "Congratulations, CAPT and Mrs. Don O'Shea, you've just given birth to a prudent money manager." These are learned skills, and **ANY ARMED FORCES MEMBER** can read, learn, understand, grasp, implement, and reap the rewards of these financial principles.

Make a promise to yourself to STOP spending on items that aren't in line with your goals, and START spending on items that are!

That's it for this edition. Please check back soon for updated stories, additions, and anecdotes.

As you can see, this guide is evolving based on the input that **YOU**, the reader, provide. So please continue e-mailing your questions, concerns, stories, and comments to Discounts@ArmedForcesFunds.com

May all of your future financial decisions continue to bring you joy and continue to enhance your lives.

Appendix A

Some Real-World Examples of Money Management Dilemmas, Goals, and Choices

The following stories are real and quite common. There are similar personnel experiencing these scenarios on your base, in your command, your office, and even your family **every day**. So please, learn to recognize these traits, and **relay a story or two** to those encountering these financial situations. If you recognize similar characteristics in yourself, seek additional information at your local base library or family assistance center. The information and qualified personnel are in place at every base, you just need to ask for assistance to get started at your personal or command level. You'll all be better off.

Franklyn

In 2002, a young man moving overseas shared his financial goals for the timeframe of his move. Franklyn mentioned he'd like to be debt-free in 3 years when he and his family return from Okinawa.

It seems like that's the goal of a lot of individuals, especially young families. It's good that he's setting some goals for himself and his family. His commitment to keeping these goals will be paramount to his achieving them, gaining confidence, and eventually setting higher goals. Now, the big question: does he have a plan?

Logically, he'll have to change his current spending habits if he wants to change his results. Has he talked with anyone who's achieved his desired results? Does he have a proven, time-tested plan to follow? Only he knows for sure.

Odds are he'll be more successful if he has a plan, and sticks to it. In the next three years, he WANTS to become debt-free. But what he REALLY WANTS is to see new things, experience a new culture, and travel while he's in that part of the world.

If he has a written plan, he'll be historically more successful finding ways to balance all of his wants. Maybe he doesn't eat dinner out as much, or spend as freely with his disposable income. By having a plan to monitor his goal, he can see how well he's progressing towards both his long and short-term goals.

By 2005, there is a happy end to this story as relayed by his father. Franklyn and his wife were blessed with a daughter to add to their family. They purchased a home in San Diego, near his next duty station. They paid down considerable "consumer" debt, and are now investing in "investment" debt by owning a home. His promotion helped, as he directed a portion of his pay increase to paying off consumer debt by following the Rule of 1/3. He is up for another promotion now, and all is well with their family as they start their next CONUS tour.

Franklyn and his family RECOGNIZED where they were financially, decided this was NOT where they wanted to be, changed course, STOPPED the habits that got them where they were (spending on consumer debt), STARTED the habits to get them to their goals from where they were (obeyed the Rule of 1/3, paid down consumer debt, bought a home with investment debt) and are ON THEIR WAY to a healthier financial retirement by respecting the laws of money.

Gordon

Back in 1982, Gordon was a thin, rather shy college student. While at school, he earned a mere $60 per month for spending money.

After college, Gordon took two steps that will serve him well for the rest of his life. He began working out his body, gradually increasing his workout routine by weight and by time. Over a few years, he added 80 pounds of muscle to his frame while increasing his endurance in his running routine. Financially, he performed equally well. Just as with his weightlifting, Gordon began investing slowly, with small amounts each month. Now, he is a financially sound investor, and keeps true to his monthly investment routine with American Century.

In 2005, Gordon updated us with additional good news. He is stationed in Saudi Arabia, an active duty Marine, and now INVESTS 76% OF HIS MONTHLY TAX-FREE EARNINGS! He redefined the Rule of 1/3 to fit his needs by foregoing additional standard of living increases, increasing his tithe, is known as a heavy tipper when he DOES dine out, and smiles each payday knowing he is dollar cost averaging his way to a secure retirement! He still invests primarily with American Century in no-load mutual funds, tracks his investments and banking online, and credits the IRS-style investment method with his tremendous financial success.

Remarkably, yet predictably, he continues to abide by the Spring Financial Cleaning philosophy, updating his documents and goals each spring on his birthday. His new goals include purchasing a home WITH CASH when he returns stateside, eventually FULLY RETIRING at age 43 with NO MORTGAGE, and enjoying life by working wherever he desires, as he is truly financially independent thanks to his planning and his military retirement income.

He earned his unique and remarkable character by following sound financial advice. THIS is the type of Marine who successfully applied his acquired character traits of honesty, integrity, accountability, drive, tenacity, and performance from his Marine career to his financial goals while remaining on active duty. We NEED MORE examples like Gordon in our society! He is a great American. You CAN do it all while remaining on active duty!

James

James has a court-ordered financial settlement coming, and he turned 18 years old in July 2002. In March 2002, he did not want to set aside some of the money for school; his intention was to put all of the money away tax-deferred, and only touch it in retirement (or early retirement, depending on his choice). He is choosing to defer his gratification until the future, and it will grow tax-deferred until he needs it.

Running the numbers, if he invested all $60k and earns 9% tax-deferred, he'll have a healthy nest egg of $2.6 million at age 60, and will even have the option of retiring earlier and taking equal and substantial payments on his money.

However, in April 2002 he changed his mind. He took some of the money and buying...a car! It's HIS money, nobody else's, but he may not fully understand the opportunity he had to secure his own future. He chose a path of buying a car and investing the remainder, and he should still be OK for retirement. But again, he chose current spending over future spending. He purchased a depreciating asset ($15,000 vehicle) for current use, and depleted his capital that could have grown towards his retirement. In effect, his options broke down as follows:

Option A – Invest all $60k, tax deferred.
At age 60, earning 9%, he'll have $2.6 million!

Option B – Invest $45k, tax deferred, and spend $15k on a car. At age 60, earning 9%, he'll have $1.9 million!

Essentially, it comes down to this; his choice to spend $15,000 on a depreciating asset (car) now cost him $700,000 in potential future value.

By 2005 James had depleted his entire account. It was his choice. He chose current spending over future financial security. THIS IS NOT RIGHT OR WRONG. It was his choice. Only HE can decide if the money was well spent. He understands where he is now financially, and knows he has unlimited potential, at the ripe age of 21, to decide WHAT he wants to do in life and how he wants to live. If he chooses to follow the laws of money he will have a bright, unlimited financial future, regardless of his current financial situation. Only he can make that choice.

Steve

Steve's story goes like this. He is married with two children, and works two jobs to make ends meet. He earns $25,000 annually at one job, which breaks down to a $462 weekly salary paid by his retail company.

When he started employment, his manager **strongly** encouraged him to automatically, via IRS-style investments method, redirect $10 weekly into his Employee Stock Ownership Plan (ESOP), which purchases discounted shares of his retail company stock. Although he was hesitant, he knew he wouldn't miss $10 per paycheck. It has now been more than FIVE years since he started this ESOP, and he has accumulated more than $7,000! How did he do it? When he received pay raises, he followed the **Rule of 1/3** and **increased** his weekly allotment by $10. Additionally, the underlying price of his shares increased, thereby providing additional value.

This disciplined savings routine will enable he and his wife to put some money down on a house when the time comes. Eventually they will buy a home, financing an appreciating asset with investment debt.

And **what made it all possible** was one retail manager taking time to stress the importance of investing a few dollars from each paycheck. **YOU** can decide to be like this retail manager. **YOU** can decide to encourage a co-worker, friend, or family member to save and invest small amounts of money this way. It makes a difference in people's lives!

Steve's experienced the pain of waking up one day and realizing the cold autumn winds are coming, so he's storing up now (saving money) to stay ahead and give himself and his family more options in the future.

By next year, Steve will have his desired downpayment. Additionally, he has learned to LIVE ON LESS THAN HE EARNS, automatically invest a portion of his income toward financial goals, and his family REAPS THE BENEFITS of these financial principals Steve's manager recommended! Incidentally, Steve is now recommending this technique to newer employees of his company so that they too may reap the benefits down the road!

Common Bonds

Isn't it amazing that there are common links between these individuals? All make choices between how much to spend now, how much to set aside for the future, and how to invest the difference.

It's straightforward, similar to taking off those few extra pounds. It isn't easy, but if you burn off more calories than you intake, you will lose weight. And if you spend less money than you earn each month, you'll set money aside for your future to earn more for you.

So please, decide where you want to be financially, commit to that goal, and then tailor your lifestyle to ensure you're on a path to meet your goal in the timeframe you desire.

Remember, **YOU** decide your goals. **YOU** commit to them. **YOU** make decisions every day on how and why you spend and invest the way you do. **YOU** can decide, through your daily financial decisions, whether you achieve your goals in your desired timeframe.

Appendix B

The Opportunity Cost of Coffee

Have you ever seen an 18-year old ordering a coffee or a latte at the local shopping mall? Here's a quick look at the OPPORTUNITY COST of buying coffee by the cup.

If our 18-year old chooses to NOT spend $3.50 on a latte, frappacino, or coffee every day, but instead invests that money into a mutual fund earning 10% annually (5% first year), growing tax-deferred, then here are the amounts he'd accumulate at various intervals. **Attention young workers – does this appeal to you?**

How much will accumulate in 5 years? How about 10 years? Can you guess what 20 years look like? Turn the page to see the answers. THIS IS IMPORTANT!

After 1 year, our now 19-year old has an account balance of **$1,323**.

After 5 years, our now 23-year old has an account balance of **$8,077**.

After 10 years, our now 28-year old has an account balance of **$21,085**.

After 20 years, our now 38-year old has an account balance of **$75,775!**

Wow.

What if you're not 18 right now? What if you're 29? Well, then at age 49, you can have an extra $75,775. The twenty-year timeframe is the same, but your age is different.

This isn't magic, it's simply the power of compound interest. Let your money work for you. YOUR SMALL DAILY FINANCIAL DECISIONS MATTER!

Now, after seeing that in a mere 20 years the non-coffee-drinker's account value is over $75,000, does that give you reason enough to consider **not** buying that coffee every day?

And, **to ensure against any bias,** the same holds true of course for soda drinkers, alcohol drinkers, and tobacco users (smokers and chewers). All of those little dollars here and there add up, so make certain you're receiving FULL VALUE for your money and think twice before spending!

Appendix C

The Daily Ledger

Once again, back by request, is an age-old, proven method to get a grip on your cash flow.

Take out a clean sheet of paper, and make the following column headings:
Date, Amount, Item Purchased, For What Purpose, Comments.

Every time you make a purchase throughout the day, mark down whom you paid, the amount, and for what purpose. Before you go to bed, record the purchases you make.

After a couple of days, you'll begin to see patterns develop. 85 cents paid to the local 7-11 for coffee every morning. $4.25 for lunch at the cafeteria. $30.00 to fill up the gas tank in the car.

But you'll also see a pattern of **spontaneous** spending versus **planned** spending. This you can record in your comments column.

For example, if you bought your normal cup of coffee, and then purchased three donuts that looked delicious, you can add the spontaneous donut spree to your comments section. Next time you buy coffee, you may **have the conversation with yourself** that gee, do you really NEED the donuts, or do you WANT the donuts? It becomes its own form of double-check on your spending.

Also, you can record WANT versus NEED items. This can help you identify what you NEED to spend (mortgage, insurance payments) versus what you WANT to spend (concert tickets, new leather jacket).

Try it for a few weeks, and if you don't see a difference in how you view spontaneous spending, then take time to double-check your annotations. Eventually, you'll see patterns, rethink some purchases, and say 'Wow, this really does work'!

Do you see what you're doing? You're **correcting** for the winds that are blowing you off course. Even Tiger Woods needs to reevaluate and correct his swing every now and then!

Appendix D – New!

How Do You Stack Up?

On average, out of 100 military personnel responding, the following statistics were attained, given a total of 1,800 random respondents:

- 53 do NOT have an up-to-date will for their state, citing lack of time and availability at their JAG office as main reasons
- 42 have NOT updated beneficiaries for retirement accounts or insurance policies in last 2 years
- 93 have NEVER searched for unclaimed property for current or previous states
- 61 do NOT have minor children's guardians identified in writing
- 37 within two years of military retirement have NO life insurance other than SGLI and spousal SGLI policies
- 19 spouses changed employers in the last 2 years but did not roll over their retirement plans
- 7 need IRAs immediately for present-year tax savings
- 61 have refinanced their current home mortgage in the last 2 years
- 77 do NOT pay extra principal on mortgage payments

- 37 did not realize veterans receive property mortgage breaks (or auto registration discounts)
- 6 receive more than $1,000 in interest or dividend payments annually
- 14 pay federal income tax on their social security income
- 11 want assistance with college planning for children or grandchildren

These numbers will vary from base to base, of course, but on the average they'll be pretty close. Do you think these personnel are better off or worse off updating their beneficiary information every spring? Do you think these personnel are better off or worse off updating their wills every year? Do you think they are better served checking their 401(k) asset allocation with an outside source every spring? Do you think they are better served having professionals double-check their tax-efficient pursuit of their financial goals? The answer is of course a resounding 'yes' to each of these questions. WE are all better off having trusted second opinions regarding any goals, whether weight loss, strength gain, quitting smoking, or building wealth, from those who have done so successfully.

Because you asked…here is the Average Net Worth for U.S. families, both by age and by pay, as of January 1, 2005.

Age	Average Net Worth
Less than 35	$ 11,400
35-44	$ 48,500
45-54	$ 90,500
55-64	$ 110,800
65-74	$ 104,100
75 and more	$ 95,000

Flip the page and you'll find the average net worth categorized by household income for all U.S. citizens. How do you stack up next to your peers?

Household Income	Average Net Worth
Less than $10,000	$ 4,800
$10,000 - $24,999	$ 30,000
$25,000 - $49,999	$ 54,900
$50,000 - $99,999	$ 121,100
Above $100,000	$ 485,900

It's worth remembering something else too. After you retire from our military, your pension is **not** included as an asset; rather, it's included in your **income** statement. Using logic, and applying the long-term risk-free rate of return of 4%, a proper net worth calculation would be fair and appropriate.

What amount of capital is required to provide an equal amount of income annually with **no risk** to the investor? Applying our 4% rate, $1,000,000 in capital invested at 4% returns $40,000 annually to an investor.

Translate this as follows: if you have a $40,000 annual pension, then essentially this represents a **one million dollar** asset that you have accumulated. If your pension is half that amount, that still represents a $500,000 asset. That puts you where you belong – **right at the top** of your peer group!

As a bonus, here is the original computer mousepad printout **from 1996** that so many of you followed to begin investing!!! It works JUST AS WELL today!

> # Have you paid yourself yet this month?

If not, we invite you to join us - **YOU CAN BE ON YOUR WAY TODAY!**

Age	Year	Rank	Base Pay	Monthly Invested	Total Invested	Cumulative Interest	Total Account Value
18	1	E-1	$875	$20	$240	$26	$266
19	2	E-2	$981	$30	$480	$54	$560
20	3	E-2	$981	$30	$720	$86	$885
21	4	E-3	$1,117	$40	$1,080	$133	$1,379
22	5	E-3	$1,162	$40	$1,440	$186	$1,925
23	6	E-4	$1,303	$60	$2,040	$270	$2,795
24	7	E-4	$1,354	$60	$2,640	$363	$3,758
25	8	E-4	$1,354	$60	$3,240	$466	$4,824
26	9	E-5	$1,532	$85	$4,140	$613	$6,337
27	10	E-5	$1,532	$85	$5,040	$774	$8,011
28	11	E-5	$1,592	$95	$5,940	$953	$9,865
29	12	E-6	$1,743	$120	$7,140	$1,184	$12,249
30	13	E-6	$1,832	$120	$8,340	$1,439	$14,888
31	14	E-6	$1,832	$135	$9,540	$1,721	$17,809
32	15	E-7	$2,112	$145	$11,040	$2,066	$21,375
33	16	E-7	$2,112	$145	$12,540	$2,448	$25,323
34	17	E-7	$2,172	$145	$14,040	$2,870	$29,693
35	18	E-7	$2,172	$160	$15,840	$3,370	$34,862
36	19	E-7	$2,232	$150	$17,640	$3,923	$40,585
37	20	E-8	$2,501	$200	$20,040	$4,599	$47,585

And here is the original computer mousepad printout **from 1996** for officers that you credit with kick-starting your investment habits. It works JUST AS WELL today!

Pay Yourself FIRST!!

Age	Year	Rank	Base Pay	Monthly Invested	Cumul Invested	Interest Earned	Total Account Value
18	1	MIDN	*	$20	$240	$19	$259
19	2	MIDN	*	$20	$480	$40	$539
20	3	MIDN	*	$20	$720	$62	$841
21	4	MIDN	*	$30	$1,080	$96	$1,298
22	5	O-1	$1,657	$50	$1,680	$152	$2,049
23	6	O-1	$1,657	$50	$2,280	$212	$2,861
24	7	O-2	$2,107	$100	$3,480	$325	$4,386
25	8	O-2	$2,532	$100	$4,680	$447	$6,033
26	9	O-3	$2,963	$150	$6,480	$627	$8,460
27	10	O-3	$2,963	$200	$8,880	$869	$11,729
28	11	O-3	$3,067	$200	$11,280	$1,130	$15,259
29	12	O-3	$3,067	$200	$13,680	$1,413	$19,072
30	13	O-3	$3,177	$200	$16,080	$1,718	$23,189
31	14	O-3	$3,177	$200	$18,480	$2,047	$27,636
32	15	O-4	$3,514	$300	$22,080	$2,499	$33,735
33	16	O-4	$3,514	$300	$25,680	$2,987	$40,322
34	17	O-4	$3,712	$300	$29,280	$3,514	$47,436
35	18	O-4	$3,712	$300	$32,880	$4,083	$55,119
36	19	O-4	$3,881	$300	$36,480	$4,698	$63,416
37	20	O-5	$4,109	$350	$40,680	$5,409	$73,026

Appendix E – New!

Pro-Military Web Resources YOU Recommend Visiting

Websites in **bold type** deserve your special attention, as they received perfect scores from MORE THAN 20 veterans who offered input on their content. Other websites received more than 5 mentions in a positive light. Any readers who wish to share their pro-military website approval for future printings please send an e-mail and share the story behind your appreciation.

www.aafmaa.org

www.afba.com

www.afbank.com

www.afi.org

www.airforcefcu.com

www.bofa.com/military

www.CincHouse.com

www.dav.org

www.dodcommunitybank.org

www.firstcommand.com

www.fool.com

www.GarrettPlanningNetwork.com

www.geico.com

www.irs.gov

www.jeacle.ie/mortgage

www.legion.org

www.LibertyTax.com

www.martindale.com

www.marinefederal.org

www.Military.com

www.militaryalmanac.com

www.MilitaryFN.com

www.MilitaryOneSource.com

www.moaa.org

www.navymutual.org

www.ncoausa.org

www.nolo.com

www.penfed.org

www.ReliaQuote.com

www.SmartMoney.com

www.socialsecurity.gov

www.suzeorman.com

www.TheHelmsman.com

www.toysfortots.org

www.trea.org

www.tricare.osd.mil

www.Unclaimed.org

www.usaa.com

www.usaaedfoundation.org

www.usna.edu

www.va.gov

www.vfw.org

Here are some quotes you offered via email to share with your brothers-in-arms.

"He who does not risk cannot win." - John Paul Jones

"Only the weak are cruel. Gentleness can only be expected from the strong." – Felice Leonardo Buscaglia

"Build me a son, O Lord, who will be strong enough to know when he is weak, and brave enough to face himself when he is afraid, one who will be proud and unbending in honest defeat, and humble and gentle in victory." - Douglas MacArthur

"If you want to launch big ships, don't be afraid of the deep water." – Grover L. Wright

"ALL of our visitors bring happiness; some by coming, others by going." - Anonymous

"One man with courage makes a majority." – Andrew Jackson

"If you don't know jewelry, know your jeweler." – Mae West

"Resolve to be tender with the young, compassionate with the aging, sympathetic with the striving and tolerant of the weak and the wrong because sometime in your life, you will have been all of these." Leo Buscaglia

"What lies beneath us, and what lies before us, are tiny matter compared to what lies within us." - Ralph Waldo Emerson

"It is the soldier, not the reporter, who has given us the freedom of the press. It is the soldier, not the poet, who has given us freedom of speech. It is the soldier, not the agitator, who has given us the freedom to protest. It is the soldier who salutes the flag, serves beneath the flag, whose coffin is draped by the flag, who gives that protester the freedom to abuse and burn that flag." - Zell Miller

"Getting knocked down is no disgrace. Staying there is." - Darrell Royal

"Nothing changes if nothing changes." - Father John

"Some people spend an entire lifetime wondering if they've made a difference to this world...our Marines don't have that problem."
- President Ronald Reagan, 1985

TODAY I vow to:

1. **Spend less money than I earn by recognizing 'Want' versus 'Need' spending**

2. **Thank myself NOW for saving towards future goals**

3. **Remember that a Part of All I Earn is MINE to KEEP!**

4. **Abide by the Rule of 1/3 for bonuses and payraises**

Please feel welcome to cut this page out and hang it on your bathroom mirror as a reminder that YOU control YOUR money, no one else does!

Index

Allotment, direct paycheck 15,16,34,35

Annuities, fixed 109,111,113,114

Asset allocation 84,148

Automating your investments 4,29,139

Bills, online paying 123-125

Bonds 82,83,99-111,123,125

Brokerage firms 74,84,114,121,123

Budgeting 18,56,125

Charitable contributions 89,137

Company retirement plans 40-42,95-98

Compound interest 144

Credit card debt 4,14-21,55-56

Consolidating 121-123,131-133

Direct deposit 14-16,55-57

Earnings 10-12,21,45-47,77-84

Exchange-Traded Funds (ETF) 34-37

Fifteen year mortgages 72

Financial advisors 35-36,64,126

Financial planning 24-27,53,121-130

Government income tax savings 114

Home purchases 18,71,100,140

Income 12,15,27,28,111,112

Income Taxes 23,31-35,112,115

Index mutual funds 33-36,123

IRAs 19,95-97,120

IRAs, Roth 27-38,95

Inheriting 80,81

Interest rates 25,68-74,109-114

IRS 15,16,99-104,137

Investments 33-39,120-133

Load mutual funds 34-36,84

Mortgage 17-18,67-74,125-128

Mutual funds 33-38,68,125-132

NASDAQ 161

No-load mutual funds 33-38,137

Online bill pay 123-125

Online resources 153-155

Pay yourself first 9-16,55-57

Pre-tax investing 29-31,88-98

Real estate 4,18,73-75

Retirement investing 113-117

Rule of 1/3 57,103,136-138,158

Savings 15-19,27-32,48-50,80-85

Spending 6-13,18-21,55-59,119-122

Tax-deferred investments 31,89,138-140

Thirty year mortgages 67-75

Thrift Savings Plan 28-32,95

Traditional IRAs, see IRAs

US government 5,28-30

VA, Dept of Veterans Affairs 124

Bibliography

Clason, George S. The Richest Man in Babylon. New York: Dutton, 1989.

Graham, Benjamin. The Intelligent Investor. New York: HarperCollins Publishing, 1973.

Kobliner, Beth. Get A Financial Life: Personal Finance In Your Twenties and Thirties. New York: Fireside, 1996

Lynch, Peter. One Up On Wall Street. New York: Fireside, 1989.

Meese, Michael et al. Armed Forces Guide to Personal Financial Planning. PA: Stackpole Books, 2002.

Palermo, Michael. AARP Crash Course in Estate Planning. New York: Sterling Publishing Co., 2004.

Rattan, James. Financial Planning and Investments for Military Personnel. CA: Naval Postgraduate School, 1975.

Rothman, Douglas. Military Survival Guide to Financial Planning. New York: N.p., 1996.

Vangeli, Arthur. Stop Buying $63 Hamburgers!. Nevada: Joe Mann Books, 2002.

Order Form for Additional Copies of "What They DON'T Teach You About Money in the Military"

And other books by Arthur J. Vangeli

Please print!

Your Name _____

Mailing Address _____

City _____ State _____

Zip Code _____ Phone (optional)_____
    (Confidentiality guaranteed. We DO NOT sell your info.)

"What They DON'T Teach You About Money…!"
                _____ copies @ $19 each $_____

"Stop Buying $63 Hamburgers!" (2002 version)
                _____ copies @ $8 each $_____

"Your Final Act of Love"
                _____ copies @ $39 each $_____

"8 Simple Rules for Financial Advisors"
                _____ copies @$1,499 each $_____

          Postage & handling @ $4.50 **per book** $_____

                Total amount enclosed $_____

Please make checks or money order payable to:
Armed Forces Funds®
11226 Woodridge Path, San Antonio, TX 78249
Discounts@ArmedForcesFunds.com Use "Books" as subject
Thank you for your patronage!